MANY HAPPY RETURNS:
THE LIVES OF EDGAR CAYCE

Many Happy Returns

THE LIVES OF EDGAR CAYCE

W. H. CHURCH

1817

Harper & Row, Publishers, San Francisco
Cambridge, Hagerstown, New York, Philadelphia
London, Mexico City, São Paulo, Singapore, Sydney

To protect the identity of those individuals, living or dead, who obtained psychic readings from Edgar Cayce and who appear in the pages of this narrative, the individual case numbers have been substituted for actual names in the present.

Extracts from the Edgar Cayce readings are identified by file reference number throughout, usually appearing in the notes at the rear of the book but sometimes incorporated in the body of the text itself. (The number to the left of the hyphen identifies the specific individual or subject, while the number following the hyphen denotes the sequence, where multiple readings have been given for that particular individual or subject.)

Chapters 8, 13, and 14 were previously published in abridged form in the *A.R.E. Journal,* under the titles "Edgar Cayce and the Siege of Troy," "The Two Lives of John Bainbridge," and "A Child of Love," respectively (issues of publication, as named: vol. XVIII, no. 5, Sept. 1983; vol. XIX, no. 1, Jan. 1984; and vol. XVI, no. 6, Nov. 1981).

Edgar Cayce readings © 1971 by the Edgar Cayce Foundation. Reprinted by permission. The quotations from the Edgar Cayce readings have been checked for accuracy by the A.R.E. The opinions expressed are those of the author and are not necessarily endorsed by A.R.E. and the Edgar Cayce Foundation.

MANY HAPPY RETURNS: *The Lives of Edgar Cayce.* Copyright © 1984 by W. H. Church. All rights reserved. Printed in the United States of America. No part of this book may be used or reproduced in any manner whatsoever without written permission except in the case of brief quotations embodied in critical articles and reviews. For information address Harper & Row, Publishers, Inc., 10 East 53rd Street, New York, NY 10022. Published simultaneously in Canada by Fitzhenry & Whiteside, Limited, Toronto.

FIRST HARPER & ROW PAPERBACK EDITION PUBLISHED IN 1986.

Library of Congress Cataloging in Publication Data
Church, W. H.
    MANY HAPPY RETURNS.
    Bibliography: p.
    1. Cayce, Edgar, 1877–1945.   2. Psychical research—United States—Biography.   3. Reincarnation—Case Studies.
I. Title.
BF1027.C3C48   1984   133.8'092'4 [B]   84–47717
ISBN 0–06–250150–X
ISBN 0-06-250151-8(pbk)

87 88 89 90 10 9 8 7 6 5 4 3 2

For Gladys, who knew him best

Contents

	Preface	*ix*
1	The Flight of the Egret	*1*
2	Unraveling the Gordian Knot	*9*
3	In the Beginning	*26*
4	When the Two Were as One	*38*
5	An Aryan in Egypt	*60*
6	Escape from Sodom	*104*
7	"O King! O Uhjltd!"	*112*
8	The Siege of Troy	*134*
9	The Sage of Samos	*148*
10	A Grecian Tableau	*161*
11	Lucius of Cyrene	*168*
12	Among the Arawaks	*179*
13	The Two Lives of John Bainbridge	*184*
14	The Love Child	*206*
15	A Civil War Vignette	*222*
16	The First Return of Edgar Cayce	*225*
17	The Second Return of Edgar Cayce	*233*
	Notes	*235*

Preface

The late American psychic Edgar Cayce probably did more than any other contemporary figure to reintroduce and popularize the ancient doctrine of reincarnation, which Western civilization had arbitrarily rejected when it decided to adopt Christianity.

Yet the notion that Christianity and reincarnation are somehow incompatible is a tragic misconception. It has created a schism where one never should have existed. For one who is willing to look, there is evidence enough in passages from both the Old and the New Testaments of the Bible to support the conclusion that not only was reincarnation a respected and commonly accepted doctrine in the days of the ancient prophets but it may well have been a doctrine accepted and taught by Jesus Himself. Certainly the apostle Paul appears to have espoused a belief in reincarnation quite openly, as is attested to in certain sayings of his about the synonymity of Adam and Jesus—and in more mystical terms, Melchizedek and Jesus, as the risen Christ.

Can any other doctrine than reincarnation and its corollary, the law of karma, so readily explain or justify the seeming inequities of the human condition in which we find ourselves? Karma, which is simply the law of cause and effect carried forward from one incarnation to another, is totally in consonance with two well-known biblical precepts: "As ye sow, so shall ye reap," and, "As the tree falls, so shall it lie."

As Edgar Cayce so succinctly put it, "The entity is ever meeting self." This was the recurrent theme in more than twenty-five hundred life readings he gave, including those given on his own past lives. There can be no better introduction to the subject of reincarnation and karma, surely, than a true narrative, such as the present one, tracing the long cyclical journey of a soul in search of its Self.

And when that soul-entity is Edgar Cayce, we are bound to gain some unique perspectives: not only was he a master of the subject, when we consider his extensive trance-state counsel to the many hundreds of people who had life readings from him over a span of several decades, but his own prior lives seem to have run the gamut from saintly priest to abject sinner, thus providing us with a rich diversity of examples of soul development and soul retrogression to study and ponder.

This story concerns a soul-entity who was unusual in many ways—perhaps older than most, and probably wiser. The reader will discover, among other things, that Edgar Cayce was blessed from the beginning with a special relationship with the Master of men. It was a relationship that inevitably shaped and colored his character and often brought him back into the earth-plane with an intensity of purpose and a selfless dedication that few of us can match or even comprehend. Not too surprisingly, one of the themes repeatedly stressed in the Edgar Cayce readings was the need to stand aside and watch self pass by. Cayce, ever fearful of the cult of personality, warned repeatedly against making a "cult" of any kind of his work here in the earth, which he felt should stand on its own and speak for itself. Above all, he eschewed any attempt on the part of well-meaning individuals to elevate him to a status above his fellow mortals. He well knew what a sinner he had been in some of his prior lifetimes and what a sinner in many respects he still was. He certainly didn't want to add to his karmic load the sin of self-glorification!

In consequence, Edgar Cayce was probably one of the most genuinely humble, self-effacing men who ever lived. Although it may be hard to maintain that image of him in light of some of the unusual revelations about his past lives and accomplishments contained in this narrative, let us remember that only those souls who have tasted greatness can come to appreciate true humility. Out of his many lives, with their multitude of lessons, Cayce had finally learned that the way to God is through self-immolation; there is no other way to reach the Higher Self, or to nurture the God-seed within us.

Finally, though the underlying philosophy of the Edgar Cayce readings is inevitably and closely linked to the Christian religion in which Edgar himself grew up and which he always practiced in an exemplary manner, it is worth noting that tolerance of other religious faiths and belief systems remained paramount in his psychic readings and in his personal life. Indeed, he had an abiding respect for that governing principle found at the root of most of the world's major religions, "The Lord thy God is One!" The spirit of this teaching was eloquently captured in metaphorical language in the following excerpt from Work Reading 254-87: "Are there not trees of oak, of ash, of pine? There are the needs of these for meeting this or that experience . . . Then, all will fill their place. Find not fault with *any,* but rather show forth as to just how good a pine, or ash, or oak, or *vine,* thou art!"

Author's Note: Here and there, throughout the narrative that follows, there inevitably occur instances wherein the information provided in the Edgar Cayce readings has been too incomplete and tenuous to provide a definite conclusion. In such cases, I have endeavored to develop the most likely and logical dénouement possible. I acknowledge, however, that others looking at the same information in the readings from a different perspective might well draw different conclusions, with an equal probability of accuracy.

1. The Flight of the Egret

The date was January 3, 1945.

A lone egret, perched on the shore of Lake Holly in Virginia Beach, Virginia, suddenly flapped its lovely, snow-white wings and rose like an omen over the Cayce residence. Slowly it circled the brown-shingled house, then disappeared toward the east—a receding white dot swallowed up in the gray, wintry mist that crouched, catlike, over the broad swell of the Atlantic Ocean.

The muffled sounds of grief, coming from a corner of the house where Gertrude Cayce was sobbing softly to herself, could barely be heard in the bedroom where her husband, Edgar, sat silently in his wheelchair, watching from the window as the snowy egret took to the air. He saw in its sudden, majestic flight a symbol of the liberated soul's departure, and in his heart he felt a great surge of rejoicing.

As he neared the end of his sixty-seventh year, the famed American psychic Edgar Cayce was physically exhausted—"burnt out," quite literally, from an overexpenditure of his own psychic energies in service to others. The tall, gaunt frame hunched in the wheelchair looked suddenly smaller than it was, and exceedingly frail. Head slightly tilted, mouth small and solemn like a wing bent down, the once-mobile face now seemed drawn and expressionless. Only in the extraordinary eyes, as blue and penetrating as ever, could one still glimpse the lively image of Edgar Cayce's former self.

In these past few years, the urgent appeals for psychic readings, as they were called, had increased severalfold as his fame increased and the war introduced new concerns for which many sought psychic answers. Mr. Cayce had found himself unable to turn away anyone who sought his help or to take the necessary periods of rest and recuperation to restore his dangerously depleted energies. Finally, he had suffered a stroke that left him partly paralyzed. In his weakened condition, the end now appeared imminent—without the intervention of a miracle.

The "miracle" for which those around him all hoped and prayed was a physical rejuvenation. The readings indicated that Edgar Cayce had once before experienced just such a bodily regeneration, through the raising of spiritual energies, during a much earlier cycle in the earth. It was during an incarnation in ancient Egypt, as the high priest Ra Ta, in the second dynasty of that particular era. At that time, the aging spiritual leader and a contingent of his loyal followers had returned from a period of exile to begin a new phase of work. (Many of them, if their individual "life" readings could be accepted as true, had now reincarnated to be with him again, as Edgar Cayce, for the furtherance of that same work, which was to aid mankind in finding the way back to the divine Source.) The resuscitated priest had not only regained his youthful vigor in that early Egyptian incarnation but had lived on for another hundred years. During that period of grace, the Great Pyramid at Gizeh was built under his direction, as high priest, with Hermes—an incarnation of the evolving Christ—as the master architect. (Actually, the famous pyramid was never designed as a tomb, as is commonly supposed, but as a temple of initiation, as well as a prophetic record in stone of coming events in the earth leading up to the end of our present century. All of this revealing information, and more, had been presented in a startling series of readings on the subject of Cayce's Egyptian incarnation.)

The notion of having lived in the earth before, or having played a significant role in the shaping of history during at least one, and perhaps as many as several, of those prior lives, had initially been very disconcerting to Mr. Cayce. A genuinely humble man, he eschewed such honors for himself; besides, he didn't know what to make of such a strange doctrine as reincarnation. His religious roots were in a typically Southern, Protestant background, noted for its rigid orthodoxy. Even the unusual nature of his psychic gifts, which had accustomed his mind to a whole new set of realities since childhood, had not quite prepared Edgar Cayce to accept, at first, what most self-respecting Christians of his acquaintance, if questioned on the subject, would have rejected with genuine abhorrence as a heathen belief system. And he would have been quick to agree that the idea of earthly recurrence, or reincarnation, did seem to be totally at odds with the tenets of the Christian faith as he had learned them.

But Edgar began to wonder: What if some of those tenets reflected a misinterpretation of the original teachings of the Christ? Was it not wholly possible that reincarnation might have been a teaching acceptable to the early church fathers, as certain scholarly sources claimed? Given the proliferation of "isms," "schisms," conflicting translations of biblical texts, and such, that had evolved from the first century onward, there at least seemed to be a logical basis for exchanging an outright rejection of reincarnation for a more tolerant form of skepticism toward that very ancient doctrine. At any rate, Edgar had learned to trust the information that came to him in trance-state through his own psychic readings. Its accuracy had been proven over and over. Moreover, it appeared to meet the highest spiritual tests, as well.

The basis for the information in his readings—unlike the less reliable pronouncements of the "mediumistic" psychic, who surrenders his or her will to become the passive channel for a "control" on the spirit-plane—had been identified as a unique process of "going within," through the use of his own etheric energies, and directly contacting the Universal Forces, without the need for an intermediary. Therefore, when faced with his first real ideological conflict, it was not too surprising that Cayce finally opted in favor of the readings and reincarnation. Besides, as a man who had made it a practice to read the Bible from cover to cover once a year, throughout his life, Edgar recalled that it contained many veiled allusions to reincarnation that the more orthodox chose to ignore. In particular, he thought of Job's haunting question: "If a man die, shall he live again?" And there was that other passage from Job, wherein the prophet appears to answer himself: "Naked came I out of my mother's womb, and naked shall I return thither." Moreover, had not the Master Himself alluded more than once to that same time-honored doctrine? First, there was His startling statement, "Before Abraham was, I *am*"—the ever-existent soul! And did He not speak plainly enough in identifying John the Baptist as a reappearance in the earth of Elijah the prophet? Also, He knew there had been rumors among the people as to His own identity as one of the ancient prophets reborn, although He neither confirmed nor denied such allegations. Yet there was Paul's meaningful reference in Corinthians to the "first" Adam and the "last" Adam. In that reference, and again in Romans 5:14, the apostle seemed to be speaking in more than mere symbols: he appeared to be identifying Jesus as a perfected incarnation of the original Adam—an interpretation, in fact, that Cayce's own readings were eventually to confirm.

As the number of life readings given by Edgar Cayce began to increase, he gradually saw that there were definite karmic patterns emerging in virtually every case. Nothing, it seemed, was by chance. Each entity in the earth was ever meeting itself and reaping the fruits of its former actions. These karmic patterns, moreover, were wholly consistent with spiritual law as presented in the Bible. The "law of karma," in fact, was really nothing more nor less than the familiar law of cause and effect, carried forward from one lifetime to the next. It was supported by two oft-quoted biblical precepts: first, "Whatsoever a man soweth, that shall he also reap," and, as its inevitable corollary, "As the tree falls, so shall it lie." Thus, the doctrine of reincarnation and karma was able to explain in properly biblical, rational terms what seemed always to have eluded the theologians—namely, the puzzling inequities of the human condition in which we all find ourselves. If the good sometimes appear to suffer for naught and the evil to go unpunished, it is only because of our limited perspective of the matter. If we could see into the past lives of the sinner and the saint, as well as the lives yet to come, we would comprehend the workings of divine justice. The judgments of God are not hurried. In His own time, He exacts from each debtor the utmost farthing and bestows upon each returning prodigal son or daughter His utmost blessing.

It is even as the psalmist sang: "He that goeth forth and weepeth, bearing precious seed, shall doubtless come again with rejoicing, bringing his sheaves with him."

Each cycle of entry into earthly consciousness, as the readings made clear, is marked by a renewed opportunity to meet and over-come any sins of omission or commission from the past. This meeting of self may be accomplished through the law of grace, as found in Him, the Redeemer, or through the law of karma and suffering, as set in the lower self and its untamed desires. All de-pends on the will of the entity, and the choices it makes each time around, until it can free itself from the wheel of death and rebirth in the realms of material consciousness. If it slips during one incar-nation, it must make up the slippage during another and another, until its failings are erased. For, the law of the Lord is perfect. Nor has He willed that any soul shall perish.

Flesh, the readings pointed out, becomes the testing portion of the universal vibration, and the earthbound souls must continue here until the human vibration accords with the divine, as in the beginning. In the case of the evolving Christ, who became our Pattern in the earth, the readings indicated that it took some thirty incarnations from His first appearance, as Adam, until His last, as Jesus, to reach a state of full attunement, or at-one-ment with the First Cause. His "resurrection" was a process of raising the fleshly vibration so that His body could resume its celestial form, or God-like condition, as a true Son of God. (And thus are we, too, gods in the making!)

We may expect, however, that it will take each one of us a similar number of lives, perhaps many more, to repeat the exam-ple of our Elder Brother, the Christ, in our cyclical evolution out of the long entrapment in the flesh. Edgar Cayce, through his dreams and readings, experienced recall of more than a dozen pri-or lives, as well as precognition of at least two earthly appearances yet to come—one in 1998, he was told, when he would re-enter as a "liberator" of oppressed mankind and another as a psychically-gifted child in Nebraska in the century following. In that latter life-time, his dream-experience indicated, he would astonish his elders by recalling intimate details of his twentieth-century appearance as the historical "sleeping prophet" of Virginia Beach.

In the interims between earthly sojourns, according to the readings, a soul-entity experiences other dimensions of consciousness. These have their equivalency in what our three-dimensional consciousness here in the earth-plane perceives as the various planetary spheres within our solar system. Such heavenly bodies as Venus, Mars, and the like certainly do exist as stellar realities, of course; but to an entity in the spiritual realm, after death, they apparently manifest a very different level of reality and rate of vibration than a three-dimensional earth-being can comprehend. Thus, in such deep metaphysical waters, it was perhaps enough to be reminded, as stated in one of the readings, that we live in a relative world, a relative universe. Here we are as babes, who must take one step at a time. As we take each step, the next is revealed to us. . . .

To Edgar Cayce now, as he sat at the window of his bedroom, monitoring the egret's rapidly vanishing flight into the eastern sky, the next step was close at hand.

His long-awaited rejuvenation was about to begin, but not quite in the manner that those around him had expected. In fact, Edgar had realized for some time now that his rejuvenation during that much earlier life in Egypt had been for a definite purpose that had no corollary in the present. His work in the earth this time around was essentially finished, with the giving of more than fourteen thousand psychic readings, which would form an inexhaustible research nucleus for generations to come. Also, he had pioneered in the establishment of holistic healing—treating body, mind, and spirit as one—as a legitimate, and sometimes near-miraculous, modality for the treatment of virtually any form of illness, including those often labeled incurable. In summary, his had been a life of continuous, unselfish service to others. Yet the next phase of the work, consisting mainly of intensive research into the material in the readings and worldwide dissemination of the findings, did not require his presence. Besides, the readings had once pointed out to Edgar that his psychic and healing activities in the earth were really the work of the Lord, by whom he had been blessed to serve as a channel. Therefore, Edgar was confident that other channels, just as worthy as himself, would be appointed to carry on when he was gone. In particular, he thought of his eldest son, Hugh Lynn, now at war in Europe, who could be relied upon to play a pivotal role in the decades immediately ahead, along with Edgar's faithful long-time secretary and friend, Gladys Davis. These two, and others, had been with him from the beginning of time, when they had all emanated from the One, projecting into the earth-plane together. As for his wife, Gertrude, who was also among that early number, Edgar already knew that it would be her soul's choice to follow him shortly to the Other Side.

Death held no fear for him, of course. He knew that life is a continuous stream of experience. Thus, to die in the material plane, as the readings had once stated it, was but to be born again into the spiritual plane. Moreover, this act of passing through God's other door, as the death-experience had been termed, was akin to the journey Edgar Cayce had taken literally thousands of times before in his out-of-body travels while giving psychic readings. All that would be different this time was that he wouldn't be returning. The silver cord must be severed at last, and the flesh-form discarded, in a process of spiritual renewal. This could be regarded as the "real" rejuvenation, and it was the one Edgar had hinted at some days previously when he had cryptically remarked to several of those close to him that they could expect to witness his complete regeneration on January fifth—a date now close at hand.

The doctor arrived as Edgar was showing signs of increasing weakness, so they moved him from his wheelchair to the bed. An oxygen mask was administered; later, however, Edgar was to push it away in a gesture of impatience. Thus did he reject any life-prolonging efforts.

At seven o'clock in the evening, Gladys was on duty at his bedside. Edgar's sister Annie entered the room with a bowlful of oyster stew. Edgar took a few sips of nourishment, then indicated that he had finished. He rested briefly. Moments later, he was dead.

The soul took its exit eastward, in the wake of the egret's earlier flight. It passed, unseen, through God's other door and came to rest in the spiritual plane, beyond the bounds of time and space.

At last the rejuvenation process could begin in earnest. And on the third day—January 5, 1945—the soul-entity's transformation was complete.

That date, not by chance, marked the holding of the funeral service in the living room of the Cayce residence on Arctic Crescent in Virginia Beach. Soon thereafter, the body would be shipped to Hopkinsville, Kentucky, for burial in the place of Cayce's birth; but now the lifeless shell lay on display in its casket. Tearful friends filed by to pay their last respects. However, those who recalled the Virginia Beach psychic's final, cryptic promise, made shortly before his death, realized that the "rejuvenated" prophet they had been told to look for on this date was not to be found in the shallow casket, where their lowered eyes rested fleetingly upon a cold, waxen figure. Rather, he was right in their midst, a warm and tangible, laughing presence. They could feel his nearness in their hearts. And in their minds, there was no doubt about it at all: Edgar Cayce was still very much *alive*.

2. Unraveling the Gordian Knot

In a wily maneuver, Alexander the Great cut the legendary Gordian knot with his sword. Thus, with a single, deft blow, he easily loosed the cord that others could not.

The author who sets out to unravel the intricate and often confusing chronology of events in the prior lives of Edgar Cayce as recorded in the readings might wish for a similarly easy way out of his dilemma. However, no verbal tricks or shortcuts will do. He knows from the outset that he must employ the legitimate skills of painstaking research and rigorous logic if he hopes to present the reader with a relatively knot-free strand of psychic rope on which to thread his story. To make the sequence of events credible, their chronology must fall into place in an orderly pattern that often seems unattainable. Yet let me see if I can offer some explanations that will set aright a number of seeming inconsistencies in a disputed handful of dates (some plainly given in the readings, others implied), while acknowledging with appropriate candor the existence of a few obvious errors of dating in the readings. These latter are not of major consequence in weighing the overall accuracy of this extraordinary psychic saga; nor do they lack a logical *raison d'être*. If we explore their probable causes, I think we can lay them properly to rest.

First, however, let me make some preliminary observations. These concern the nature of the readings themselves, with particular emphasis on their unique characteristics and relative accuracy.

When Edgar Cayce wanted to give a psychic reading, he would first loosen his clothing, such as his belt, necktie, shirtcuffs, and shoelaces, to ensure a perfectly free-flowing circulation. Then, if the reading was to be a physical one—relating to the psychic diagnosis and recommended treatment of a bodily ailment, for example—he would lie down on the couch in his office with his head to the north and his feet to the south. However, if it was to be a life reading—probing the soul records of an entity from the beginning of time—just the opposite polarization was observed. This alternating position had been recommended in one of the readings, although no one had troubled to inquire why. Conceivably, it related to the directional flow of etheronic wave forces in the atmosphere, as I shall try to explain. These waves of energy, sometimes identified in occult literature as *prāna* or *akasha,* apparently permeate the entire universe and were characterized in one of the Edgar Cayce readings as being of a "mental" nature. Thus, Cayce may have utilized these same energy currents, much as one would tune in on certain radio wavelengths, to "pick up" information on the etheric plane, whether transmitted from terrestrial or cosmic sources. But why the reverse polarization—south–north, rather than north–south—when giving a life reading as opposed to a physical reading? Could it be that etheronic currents of a cosmic nature, as they enter earth's atmosphere, flow in one direction, while those of terrestrial origin flow in another? And did the two different types of readings utilize opposing streams of energy? It would appear to be a reasonable hypothesis.

One is reminded, in fact, of a nearly identical theory propounded by André Bovis, a remarkable Frenchman who, in the earlier part of this century, impressed scientific and occult circles alike with his pioneering work on geomagnetic currents as well as the strange energy fields associated with pyramid structures. Bovis believed that the earth has positive magnetic currents running north to south and attributed an east-west flow to negative magnetic currents. But of special interest, we find, was his claim that *"any* body placed in a north–south position will be more or less polarized"[1]—a statement that certainly ties in neatly with Cayce's unique orientation, regardless of which end his head happened to be occupying. Moreover, if we follow Bovis's theory a bit further, in respect to what purportedly takes place in a north–south polarized human body, we may unravel a mystery; for in such a body, we are told, "telluric [earthly] currents, both positive and negative, enter through one leg and go out through the opposite hand. At the same time, cosmic currrents from beyond the earth enter through the other hand and foot. The currents also go out through the open eyes."[2] If we can assume, as I think we can, a symbiotic relationship of some sort, or possibly even an esoteric synonymity, between Bovis's oppositely flowing "magnetic" currents of cosmic and terrestrial origin and Cayce's "etheronic wave forces," perhaps we not only will have discovered why Cayce had to reverse his north–south polarization depending upon the type of psychic reading he was giving but will also have laid the groundwork for a better understanding of the operation of psychic phenomena in general. At any rate, it seems reasonable to hypothesize at this juncture that the telluric currents would provide an ideal medium for the conveyance of psychic intelligence on matters of an earthly or physical nature, whereas one would presumably have to "tune in" to cosmic currents to pick up the transmission of the akashic or "soul" records of an entity. If the picture is sometimes blurred or the sound garbled, it is possibly due to local static in the form of physical tiredness on the part of the psychic, improper spiritual preparation for the reading, or mental interference from others. (Such explanations, at any rate, were among those offered by the sleeping Cayce when the subject of inaccurate information in the readings came up—a subject to which we shall return in due time. It plays a crucial role in determining the right choice to make among certain conflicting dates in our psychic saga of the lives of Edgar Cayce.)

Meanwhile, now that the question of polarization is behind us, it is time to go back to the couch in Mr. Cayce's office. We had left him there in a reclining position, relaxed and ready for a psychic session.

Actually, the so-called sleep-state into which Edgar would voluntarily place himself for the giving of a reading (following a suggestion from the conductor, who was usually his wife, Gertrude), has been improperly termed a hypnotic condition. An Indian authority on the subject, Dr. I. C. Sharma, sets us straight: "This sleep-state," he writes, "is actually what the mystics call

Turiya Avastha, or the state of transcendental sleep–consciousness. In this state, which is usually induced voluntarily through the practice of meditation and spiritual self-discipline, the human psyche makes contact with the Cosmic Consciousness and gains knowledge which is not limited by time and space." With specific reference to Edgar Cayce, Sharma adds his view that "his spontaneous mystic ability was the result of the accumulated tendencies of previous incarnations," so that it is therefore "more appropriate to call him a pragmatic mystic than a psychic or hypnotic or sleeping prophet."[3]

Yet another perspective on Cayce's unique psychic ability was volunteered in a trance session given in 1934 by the well-known English mediumistic psychic Eileen Garrett, whose "control" was identified as an Arab named Uvani, dwelling on the "fifth plane."

Uvani, speaking through Mrs. Garrett, explained that Edgar Cayce was "using his full etheric leverage," actually passing into the etheric state when giving a reading, so that he was, as it were, "outside of his body." He was also "drawing upon his own spiritual light" to assist others, "giving you something of his own life. This is what happens."[4]

Uvani acknowledged that Cayce's unusual psychic abilities also depended to a large degree upon the high level of development he had reached in previous incarnations. "Unless he had indeed understood in the past the laws of passivity, the laws of withdrawal, and the inner law of knowing," Uvani explained, "he would not be able to get this reflection through himself," for "he uses his own spirit reflection to see, to hear and to understand."[5]

Referring to the drain on Edgar Cayce's etheric energies, however, Uvani then proposed that Cayce permit him, or other "controls" on his plane of development, to use him as a channel for expression rather than going directly into the etheric plane himself for the information in his readings. As an enticement, he intimated that the language of the readings would come through more clearly with the aid of a helper on the spirit-plane. But later, in a check-reading on Uvani's counsel, not only was there a warning against asking help from those on this or that plane, but it was made clear that Cayce's established method of "turning within" for psychic guidance was to remain unchanged. In fact, on the same date as the check-reading (February 6, 1934), Work Reading 254–71 laid the whole matter unequivocally to rest. On that latter occasion, the sleeping Cayce was specifically asked whether it would be advisable for him to seek the sort of spirit-world assistance that "Uvani claims will increase the coherence and power of the readings." The answer took the form of a pointed question: "Does Uvani claim to know better than the Master who made him?"

No further comment was required.

In that same reading, moreover, the work of Edgar Cayce was defined as "the work of the *Master* of masters." Those around Cayce were all sufficiently humbled by that remark to leave the advice of any mediumistic psychics alone, after that. If Cayce's direct method of approach to the Universal Forces sometimes resulted in jumbled syntax or nebulous phrasing, for one reason or another, that occasional drawback in the readings was of far less serious consequence, surely, than even the best-articulated remarks of a spirit control would be, whose sources and motivation could not be verified or whose level of spiritual development was in all probability inferior to Cayce's.

Edgar's own explanation of his entry into the etheric plane to give a reading was contained in a subsequently published lecture. He tells us how he prepared himself spiritually, through prayer, then awaited guidance from an inward spark of light:

Once lying comfortably, I put both hands up to my forehead, on the spot where observers have told me that the third eye is located, and pray. Interestingly enough, I have unconsciously and instinctively, from the very beginning, adopted the practices used by initiates in meditation. This instinctive putting of my hands to the point midway between my two eyes on my forehead is a case of what I mean.

Then I wait for a few minutes, until I receive what might be called the 'go signal'—a flash of brilliant white light, sometimes tending towards the golden in color. This light is to me the sign that I have made contact. When I do not see it, I know I cannot give the reading.

After seeing the light I move my two hands down to the solar plexus, and—they tell me—my breathing now becomes very deep and rhythmic, from the diaphragm. This goes on for several minutes. When my eyes begin to flutter closed (up till now they have been open, but glazed) the conductor knows I am ready to receive the suggestion [for the reading].[6]

We come, now, to the question of relative accuracy in the readings.

Any impartial researcher into the voluminous body of transcripts on file with the Edgar Cayce Foundation and its affiliate organization, the Association for Research and Enlightenment, at Virginia Beach, covering more than fourteen thousand psychic readings given by Edgar Cayce, will have been properly impressed by one aspect, in particular—the never-ending validation process. I refer to the innumerable written testimonials and other supportive documents, as well as pertinent news clippings and updated research notes, appended to the various readings. These appear to confirm the high degree of accuracy Cayce achieved in all those areas where verification of his psychic powers has been available to date. Most notably, this applies to the physical readings, where his psychic diagnosis and recommended treatment of all manner of physical ailments often went contrary to the prevalent views of medical science at the time or to the specific advice of the attending physician in the case. Nevertheless, if doctor and patient could be persuaded to accept his diagnosis and follow his proposed treatment along the holistic lines that were uniquely Cayce's, the results were almost invariably positive and sometimes quite dramatic indeed. Similarly, Cayce's excellent track record as a New Age prophet of distinction continues, as the number of "hits" still accumulates. It is expected that this will be the case right through the end of this century, if major earth changes and other momentous events take place as the Virginia Beach seer predicted. Also, Cayce's psychic work in dream interpretation bore confirmatory fruit on quite a number of occasions throughout his lifetime. Yet, verification of the life readings, each with its record of multiple incarnations, has obviously proved to be more difficult. Only in isolated instances could certain scraps of evidence be uncovered—a tombstone or a historical document, perhaps—to lend validation to one or more of an entity's prior incarnations in the earth. However, in suggesting how one's former-life achievements could be put to the best vocational use in the present, Cayce often hit the nail on the head with an uncanny precision. Confirmation in this area still continues to mount, as the correspondence with younger recipients of life readings is added to the files.

Mostly, however, for those who had life readings it was a matter of accepting the information pretty much "on faith," or perhaps because of the sustaining threads of consistency that seemed to run through the various prior lives reported. There was also the convincingly logical relationship of past developments or failures to unfolding opportunities or restrictions in the present incarnation. (Surely no charlatan could have been gifted with sufficient imagination and sheer inventiveness to have spun such intricate life-patterns as Cayce's life readings revealed, with their complex interplay of karmic forces from one incarnation to the next!)

At the same time, it must be acknowledged that the sleeping seer had "good days" and "bad days"—days when the clarity and detail of a reading would be truly remarkable and other times when the phrasing would be exasperatingly indistinct and ambiguous, even self-contradictory here and there. Dates, and even names, would sometimes appear to be misstated, and occasionally certain segments of the information appeared to be out of proper chronological sequence.

Why?

Cayce himself has provided us with the best answers, which usually appeared in response to questions asked of him in trance-state over the years.

In a reading given in 1919, for instance, he was asked: "Is this information always correct?"[7] He replied that it was correct insofar as the suggestion was in the proper channel. This meant that the seeker not only had to provide the conductor of the reading with the correct specifics on the information being sought, in an articulate manner, but had to be properly motivated. A "proper" motivation for a life reading could be defined as a desire to obtain greater self-knowledge for purposes of soul development. Mere curiosity, as another reading pointedly remarked, was not enough.[8] Similarly, any form of self-aggrandizement on the part of the seeker would inevitably produce unsatisfying results. A spiritual goal, by contrast (as exhibited in the Search for God series of psychic readings, for example), always seemed to produce readings of outstanding quality and general clarity. Readings in this special category, in fact, have become the pillars on which the chronological structure of my story has been made to rest, wherever conflicting dates appear.

Reading 294–197, approaching the question of accuracy in the readings from another angle, warned that "there should not be the attempts to induce or to give information for others when physical hindrances arise," thus intimating that periods of ill health or physical tiredness on Edgar Cayce's part would have a deleterious impact upon his psychic forces, affecting the clarity or accuracy of a reading given under such unfavorable circumstances.

The most complete explanation of psychic errors or lapses, however, was contained in a detailed reading on the subject given in 1933.[9] In summary, it listed several causes, one of which was the unwillingness of the body-consciousness of either Edgar Cayce or the recipient of the reading to be properly responsive at the time. Another stated cause was ill health, which we have already covered. A third was the mental attitude of those in Edgar Cayce's presence at the time the information was being sought, as well as "combative influences" in the experience of the entity seeking. In this regard, specific reference was made to "the continual warring" between the flesh and the spirit. Apparently the fleshly consciousness of the seeker, in such an instance, would be endeavoring to exert its restrictive control "through such a period of information passing from one realm to another." The akashic records of a soul-entity, said the reading, are either positive or negative—negative being "error," positive being "good." But in attuning the forces at the psychic level for "reading back" the record that has been made, how does the information come? Cayce answered that question with another: "For what purpose is the information being sought?" On that philosophical note, the matter came to rest.

Quite another dimension of the subject came to light, however, in Reading 1100–26, in which Cayce actually interrupted his account of the entity's Egyptian incarnation in the time of Ra Ta to volunteer a revealing "aside." As if to explain to his conscious-state audience the frustrations he was then encountering in his unconscious state, he told them that the interpreting of the records was not from English or from the Egyptian language but from the language that the entity's people had brought into the land of Egypt with them. This, he went on to explain, was "not Sanskrit, not the early Persian," but apparently the Carpathian dialect. (At a time in man's ancient history when there was but one language common to all, as confirmed both in Genesis and in the Cayce readings, any notable language differences would presumably have been those of dialect only.)

At any rate, we can readily imagine what a monumental task must have confronted Cayce in giving some twenty-five hundred life readings throughout his career as a psychic. Operating strictly on his own, without benefit of a "control" in the spirit realm to translate on his behalf, he was obliged to project himself into the etheric plane and personally "read" the akashic records of an entity's prior lives in whatever language might apply to each of its many cycles in the earth-plane—often dating back to Lemurian or Atlantean times—right up to the present. (The keeper of the records, though, would usually withhold from his cognizance any prior lives of a soul-entity that did not pertain to that entity's present phase of soul development in the earth. This again demonstrated an emphasis on the constructive purpose of a life reading, which was spiritual in its essence, as opposed to the mere satisfying of human curiosity in probing into one's past lives.)

When we contemplate the horrendous language hurdle alone, it seems obvious that it must have accounted for at least some of the garbled phrasing and psychic misinformation that occasionally slipped into Edgar Cayce's transliterations of the akashic records. Dates or other figures would have been particularly vulnerable to misinterpretation, one supposes. And in the final analysis, one can only marvel at the overall clarity and consistency of those twenty-five hundred or so life readings given against such overwhelming odds.

This brings us to the question of disputed chronology. It is not a simple matter to resolve. It must be viewed in the larger context of virtually all of the life readings, not those pertaining to Cayce alone.

Let me explain.

A unique aspect of the Edgar Cayce readings is the way literally hundreds of people were drawn to the Virginia Beach psychic over the years, seemingly by chance, and eventually had life readings from him. (This does not include the thousands who came for physical readings only.) In their life readings, they nearly all discovered the existence of karmic bonds—some quite ancient, others of more recent origin—linking them to Edgar Cayce, for weal or woe. Many had been with him in his early Egyptian incarnation as the high priest Ra (or Ra Ta), a cycle that was being re-enacted in many ways in the present, Cayce was told, and was to have a special influence on his current role in the earth as the forerunner of a "new order" about to unfold, with the advent of a new age and a new root race at the turn of this century. Others from that same special group in the days of Ra had also reincarnated with him in a later cycle in Persia, when Cayce had been a nomadic ruler, teacher, and healer named Uhjltd, who perhaps left his major mark on mankind with the birth of a son named Zend whose offspring was Zoroaster. Zend himself, according to the readings, had been an early incarnation of Jesus. And those soul-entities who had been with Cayce in both his Egyptian and Persian cycles now tended to form, for the most part, a natural and close-knit nucleus about him in the present. It was as if they had entered the earth with an inherent awareness of their unique opportunities for further service to mankind at this special time, and in association with that same soul-entity who had led them in the past.

Yet others had been with Cayce in Troy, in Greece, or in the Holy Land; in France, in England, or in America, through later life-cycles; some sharing in those periods that had led to soul retrogression for Cayce, rather than soul development, or in periods of wavering between the two extremes, as in his incarnation in the early Christian epoch as Lucius.

Throughout all these various life expressions, however, the threads of karma—good or bad—had woven a common tapestry of crisscrossing lives and destinies, a vast mosaic of human action and interaction played out in recurring cycles on the stage of life. Now, in the present century, the ancient drama had reached a point of climax, as all of the actors were brought on stage again, some singly, others in clusters, to reap what had been sown in the past. The time for the harvest was at hand, and all were called, but only some appeared ready.

This conglomerate of soul-entities drawn to Edgar Cayce over the years, and given life readings, could be viewed quite appropriately in one sense as a single unit, an aggregate, an inseparable "soul cluster" of disparate but related cells. Like the various cells in a body, they each have a unique role to fulfill, either in harmony with their fellow cells or not, as they choose. As our story unfolds down through the aeons, we will see some of their number entering again and again, as if in joyous preparation for the present incarnation, always responding to their opportunities for soul growth and service to others. But there are also those "rebellious cells" in the cluster. Some, like Cayce himself in more than one of his incarnations, have only temporarily fallen out of step to learn a needed lesson here and there; they will return, purged and stronger. Others stumble repeatedly, tripping on the hard rocks of their own self-interest. These form a constant cutting-edge to themselves and others. It is not our role to judge them. They move more or less flamboyantly onto the stage and take a more or less hasty exit from our view.

Throughout, we are being presented with a frequent retelling of the different life-cycles of Edgar Cayce, as viewed briefly through the lives and actions of others who, in most instances, were also present in several of those same cycles. Events often take on a quite different shading or coloration as each of these numerous actors marches across the stage of history to his or her own drumbeat. We must sift, select, and discriminate among the bits and pieces of information dropped along the way until we have reassembled the threads of the tapestry into a historical likeness as near to the original as possible. Faced with the enormity of our task and its apparent limitations, there are frustrating moments. Yet we are often helped along, unwittingly and unexpectedly, by what may first appear as hindrances, for seemingly disparate threads have a curious way of matching up or blending with the rest. As a case in point, though not directly related to our story, there was the identification of two separate individuals in their life readings as the same biblical character, Gamaliel, who will be remembered as a leader of the Sanhedrin in the days of Jesus. One of these, Mr. [1188], was told that he had lived "in the days when the Master walked the land," but so had the other, Mr. [933], been told that his existence had been "when the Master was in the earth." All of the evidence pointed to an embarrassing duplication. But in that case, which was the "real"Gamaliel? As it turned out, *both* were entitled to the name given, having existed in a father and son relationship that history has largely ignored. It took some meticulous research to locate the records on Gamaliel the Second, who was born during the Master's lifetime. Not only was Cayce vindicated, but we found that his character analysis of the two Gamaliels in their separate readings served to differentiate them unmistakably.[10]

Such luck, however, is not always with the researcher; nor is impeccable accuracy, as already pointed out in the preceding pages, always characteristic of the readings. It is important to acknowledge the flaws, whatever their cause. Yet we must be sure they are flaws, not simply misreadings on our part. This is the point I have wished to stress in telling the Gamaliel story. Superficial evidence may sometimes suggest a psychic gaffe, whereas subsequent research or historical developments can serve to reverse the earlier misjudgment. For this reason, the Cayce material must be approached with an open mind and a great deal of cautious respect by any researcher. He may be forced to eat crow if he is not careful. (I have done so myself!)

With that qualification in print, I proceed.

In Cayce's Egyptian cycle as the high priest Ra, the conflicting dates encountered are quite problematical. Some are obviously in error. Which ones? In sifting and sorting through an extremely large body of readings relating to the many participants in that major era, this researcher found it advisable to establish a particular dating or two as the most reliable and work from there. After that, any readings for the various actors in the drama that introduced dates in conflict with the established "master" dates for the period as a whole simply had to be brought into conformity. Fortunately, as with the 11,016 B.C. birthdate given for the young king, Araaraart, ruler in the second dynasty, it was possible to demonstrate its inaccuracy by cross-checking it with more than one reference point. First, there was one of our "master" dates, the one-hundred-year time frame for the construction of the Great Pyramid, from 10,490 to 10,390 B.C., as given in one of the most lucid and reliable of all the readings on the period. The pyramid's construction had begun, we knew, while Araaraart was still alive. Secondly, since Araaraart's life span had been given as only 114 years, it was obvious that he could not have been born in 11,016 B.C.—526 years before the pyramid's construction commenced. Nor could he logically have been referred to as "the young king" at the time of Ra's exile to the Libyan mount, some nine years earlier than that. Finally, we located half a dozen different references to 10,500 B.C. as the "general" time frame for the Ra Ta period, which was in conformity with that pyramid dating in Reading 5748–6.

Thus, with persistent effort, the knotty chronological threads of our story of the many lives of Edgar Cayce began slowly to unravel, leaving only an occasional unresolved kink in the total strand.

Perhaps the thorniest of the chronological conundrums encountered along the way was the establishment of a probable time frame for Cayce's Persian cycle as Uhjltd, the nomadic ruler. No specific date had been given anywhere, to our knowledge, although there were several unmistakable allusions to its relative proximity to the Egyptian cycle that had preceded it. One of these was a statement to the effect that Uhjltd was the offspring of one of the daughters of Ra (Ra Ta), in union with a son of Zu. (But both "Zu" and "Ra," in this context, may have been tribal designations only. At any rate, the mother of Ra had been identified as a daughter of Zu in one of the readings on Cayce's memorable Egyptian period.) Next, one must not discount the possibility that Uhjltd may not have been a *direct* offspring of the union mentioned but simply a lineal descendant thereof. Even so, this could hardly be expected to place Uhjltd's advent very far removed from the days of Ra, in all likelihood. A thousand years or so, say? Perhaps, but not much more. For there were other readings implying a "quick return" to the earth-plane from the Egyptian cycle to the Persian one. In the context of the times, when a life span could be several hundred years, we might reasonably allow a millennium or so from the close of one earth-cycle to the birth into the next as a relatively "quick" return; a much longer span, however, would seem to stretch the taffy of credibility rather thin, catching us in a sticky situation.

Yet, a quite contrary view of the historicity of the Uhjltd era has won some adherents among students of the Cayce readings. This dissident view, moreover, is not without its logic. How to cope with it was our question. The readings on Cayce's life as Uhjltd had disclosed, as mentioned earlier in this chapter, that he was the father of Zend, an incarnation of the Master, and Zend was named as the father of Zoroaster. Now, just when the prophet Zoroaster lived has remained an historical enigma to this day. Most authorities place his advent betweeen the seventh and sixth centuries B.C. This doesn't make them right, of course. Manly Palmer Hall, the pre-eminent scholar in such matters, says no reliable information is available. In fact, he states that Zoroaster's arrival in the earth "is variously placed from the 10th to the first millennium B.C.," adding that "this uncertainty results, in part at least, from the destruction of the libraries of the Magian philosophers by the armies of Alexander the Great."[11] Meanwhile, in an Eileen Garrett reading[12] there is an intriguing reference by Uvani to "the *first* Zoroaster" (italics added), thus clearly implying that there had been at least two—the latter a namesake who could conceivably have revived the teachings of the original Zoroaster and may even have been the same entity in a much later incarnation. (For thus does history tend to repeat itself, moving in cycles down through the ages. We shall see ample evidence of it in the chapters ahead.)

However, a monkey wrench now comes hurtling toward our chronological structure from a quite unexpected source: the readings themselves. In a couple of the Cayce readings (1097–2 and 3356–1), one finds, in the one instance, an incarnation in the Persian period seeming to occur *after* an incarnation in the days of Moses (ca. 1300 B.C.) and, in the other, judging by its given sequence in the reading, even appearing later than the Babylonian exile of the Israelites (ca. 600 B.C.). Yet it is my conclusion, based on the impressive evidence in the readings to support a far earlier time frame for the Uhjltd period, that those two disputed incarnations in Readings 1097–2 and 3356–1, respectively, were simply given out of chronological sequence. No dates appear in either reading, and it is the sequence factor alone that has led to certain historical assumptions that are at odds with more convincing evidence pointing to a time frame nearer to 8000 or 9000 B.C. for Cayce's Persian incarnation as Uhjltd.

Actually, other examples of incarnations given out of sequence may be found in the readings. One of these, contained in Reading 2892–2, originally led to a great deal of needless confusion and controversy until Edgar Cayce's secretary, Gladys Davis Turner, eventually resolved the mix-up.[13] Moreover, it will be found that the life readings do not invariably begin a review of prior lives from the last appearance in the earth to the earliest, but sometimes in reverse sequence. So one should not discount the very real possibility of an occasional sequential mix-up, accidental or otherwise, as typified, for instance, in the "reverse" run-through of prior lives in Reading 5249–1.

Finally, with specific reference to our subject, Reading 288–29 gives us a further clue as to the ancient origins of the Uhjltd epoch, predating the days of Moses, if not those of Abraham as well. Referring to the Master's appearance as Zend, a son of Uhjltd, it is plainly stated: "No Jews then! That was years later!"

How many years later is the critical question. Abraham was the forefather of the Jewish people, and his days may have been roughly contemporaneous with those of Uhjltd. He dwelt at Ur, "on the other side of the flood," and some ten generations removed from Noah. And Noah? He was the great-grandson of Enoch, whose synonymity with the legendary Hermes, master architect of the Great Pyramid, we shall explore in Chapter 5, dealing with the Ra Ta period in Egypt.

Another knotty cycle in the lives of Edgar Cayce, chronologically considered, is the dual Bainbridge incarnation. For it seems that he chose to incarnate not once, but *twice,* under the same name, with the second appearance occurring approximately one hundred years later but in much the same environs and the same sort of squandered life as the former, carrying him from England as a youth to the adventurous shores of early America. In the second appearance, however, the readings stated that he had made his entrance into the earth-plane from Saturn's forces. This told me much. Saturn, according to the readings, is that nondimensional sphere of consciousness where all memory of the immediate past is wiped out—erased—so that an entity may start over again. It is like the legendary Lethe, river of forgetfulness. The soul-entity is provided with a clean slate and an opportunity to redeem itself in its next cycle of incarnation through the application of free will and choice. This explains the second appearance of John Bainbridge.

In the chapters that follow, the reader will find numerous other examples of questionable chronology or story line with which I have had to wrestle. But, aided sometimes by logic and as often by luck, I believe I have managed to unravel the snarls in most cases. If the reader disagrees with certain of my deductions and conclusions along the way, that is a privilege of which I would not deprive him or her. But at least it will be apparent, I hope, that I have aimed at presenting the full, unvarnished facts. No dates, names, or events in disagreement with my version have been intentionally hidden from the reader's scrutiny. If they are not there, and may be said to bear more than passing significance in putting the chronology aright or nailing down other specifics of the story, it is because I have inadvertently overlooked them.

At the same time, mine does not pretend to be an epic tale of grandiose proportions. It is but a skeletal framework by comparison. Its modest objective, within that framework, is to provide the essential verities in the many lives of Edgar Cayce, but not to overburden the reader with the minutiae of detail that a full-blown, traditional epic would require. If this is disappointing to some, I am sorry. Others, no doubt, will be relieved. I have spared them a thousand pages of laborious prose, for which they should be properly thankful.

Finally, let it be noted that this tale, even when it may manage occasionally to be entertaining, is always true. And the truth, as we all know, invariably conceals a moral. The moral at the core of this story is simple: Live joyously! Though the soul's long journey through the earth may often be difficult, as illustrated by Cayce's many incarnations here (with some still to come!), its goal is eventual liberation from the lower self and the restoration of the soul's lost godhood. That is surely cause for abundant joy. And so we express our earthly hope: "Many happy returns!"

Humor, not surprisingly, was always a vital undercurrent in the Edgar Cayce readings. Cayce frequently enjoined people to laugh more, to take themselves less seriously. Even the Master, he said, joked on the way to Calvary, as He carried His own cross.

Rejoice, then! Live every moment joyously. Joy is contagious. Man first got it from the angels. The angels are constantly rejoicing. The angel in man is the joy he entertains and sheds upon others. Joy awakens the Higher Self within us. And when the Higher Self awakens, we are free.

3. In the Beginning

Following the bead of light, as he always did, Edgar Cayce found himself propelled swiftly upward. Looking neither left nor right, he passed unhindered through the lower realms of relative darkness, where hordes of lost and despairing spirit-entities sought to hamper his ascent with their loud lamentations. Instead, he rose quickly into the increasing light and beauty of ever-higher levels of the spirit-plane. Here luminous beings reached out helpfully, as if to aid his upward passage. At last he came to the familiar hall of the akashic records, which was his goal.

The ageless keeper of the records recognized him. He greeted Edgar as an old friend.

"You come again," he said, smiling. "I have been expecting you."

Edgar nodded at the white-robed, turbaned figure, returning the smile. But before he could tell the akashic guardian that this time he had come for a look at his own records rather than those of another, his friend had vanished.

Yet he reappeared just as suddenly, like a beam of celestial light. In his hands he carried an unusually large tome. This suggested that it must contain the records of a very old soul—one whose journeys into the earth-plane possibly dated from the beginning of time. Emblazoned on the book's cover were curious markings, which Edgar intuitively recognized at once as his own soul number (for every entity in the earth is thus identified).

As he opened the book, Edgar saw that certain passages had been rendered indecipherable to him. And he knew this meant that he was not to receive full knowledge, as yet, of his many prior lives. His own Higher Self, in fact, had decreed these limitations. Only those pages that would prove helpful to his present phase of soul development were to be revealed to him. It was in accord with the universal laws.

Using his inner eye, Edgar read as much as was permitted him. Then he repeated the passages aloud, translating from the akashic form, and sometimes interjecting side comments of his own, in what frequently sounded like the archaic English of the King James version of the Bible, a book whose words were always sacred to him and a part of his innermost being. This process of vocalization was necessary, of course, so that those in the earth-plane, waiting in the room where his physical body rested, would be able to pick up the message in the akashic records from his unconscious, or superconscious, self.

At last he came to the earliest entry (for he had read the record from last to first, as he usually did). And those who now listened intently in the room where his body lay were transfixed by what they heard as the moving lips and tongue of the supine figure formed these revealing words, in a poetic translation from the akashic:

We find [the entity] in the beginning, when the first of the elements were given, and the forces set in motion that brought about the sphere as we find called earth-plane, and when the morning stars sang together, and the whispering winds brought the news of the coming of man's indwelling, of the spirit of the Creator, and he, man, became the living soul. (294–8)

A living soul, yes. But not yet a mortal, with a mortal's limitations.

Those who chose to enter into the earth-plane in that first influx of souls were celestial beings. They were the as-yet-unfallen sons and daughters of God, the First Cause and Creator. Their appearance was more in the nature of thought-forms, initially, that could be projected or crystallized into a bodily manifestation, as desired. It was simply a matter of visualization. Cocreators in their own right, they could draw upon the Creative Forces to translate mental images into material shape and substance through a change, or lowering, in the vibratory rate of the thought-pattern. For they were fully conscious of the Universal Mind as the builder. This application of spiritual law not only governed their own physical projections but met all of their material wants and needs in the earth-plane. (For, verily, thoughts are *things*.)

An aspect of their androgynous God-nature was the ability to separate, like the amoeba, and create a "companion self" at will. In this manner, they retained their spiritual purity, at first, holding to the celestial form but in a translated, visible state suited to an earthly experience, with its lower vibratory rate. They did not yet choose to engage in the tempting delights of fleshly copulation, as they witnessed all around them in the lustful antics of the multifarious creatures of the animal kingdom, whose appearance in the earth-plane had preceded their own.

Although now separated partially from their divine Source, they retained close psychic contact and continued to manifest the power of gods. Their deeds in the earth were to become the stuff of legends among later arrivals. And while they were indeed the true progenitors of Adamic man, who was to follow them in a later epoch, with the second influx of souls (including many of their own number, returning), man's lowly estate had not yet befallen these early, Olympian-like extraterrestrials. Their pristine forms were still essentially etheric, projected into material shape or withdrawn at will. Innocence illumined their brows with an innate nobility. Not yet were they wholly trapped in hardened, material encasements, as would be their fate later on. Not yet had the temptations of the flesh corrupted them or the ways of selfishness begun to lead them astray. For they knew not sin. Not yet, not yet . . .

Edgar Cayce was among that early number.

All souls emanate from the One, and they return to the One.

The soul's purpose in the earth, then, is to find its way back from whence it came, exercising the divine gift of free will to grow heavenward—or to separate itself further from its Maker.

And who is its Maker?

The first-begotten Son of God is identified in ancient tradition as the Upper Adam, or archetypal man, who preceded the earthly Adam and the material creation. In fact, it was He, as a god in His own right (for was He not made a full companion and heir of the Ineffable One?), who later became the Maker, the Creator, of the manifest universe. He is also identified as Mind, Light, the Word. The readings call Him Amilius, the name under which He first entered the earth-plane as a thought-form in the beginning, and through whom all the other souls were projected in that first influx, as well as in the second. Yet in the first cycle they came as gods, or celestial beings, whereas in the second they entered as flesh-form souls, or earthly man.

Surprisingly, the readings indicate that this same Amilius was led astray, so that He ultimately had to work out His own salvation in the earth, as well as preparing the Way for ours. For "this first-begotten of the Father," as the matter is explained in Reading 364–8, "allowed himself to be led in the ways of selfishness." In fact, although the soul's well-intentioned purpose here originally, as stated in Reading 341–8, was to "make manifest Heaven and Heaven's forces" in the material creation, actually the whole manifest universe and the physical entry into same marked an apparent act of disobedience.

It is a subject hard to comprehend. In fact, the sleeping Cayce readily admitted that it might even involve "too much knowledge for some"; yet I quote this question-and-answer explanation from one of the Search for God readings for the benefit of those who must have a logical interpretation of the matter. After all, it is a question that epitomizes the human dilemma, and its answer serves to clarify what reincarnation and soul development are all about:

Q–2. Please explain the following from [Reading 262–96], May 24, 1936: "For the soul had understanding before he partook of the flesh in which the choice was to be made." Why (if the soul had understanding) the necessity to take [on] flesh in order to make the choice?

A–2. Considereth thou that Spirit hath its manifestations, or does it use manifestations for its activity? The Spirit of God is aware through activity, and we see it in those things celestial, terrestrial, of the air, of all forms. And *all* of these are merely manifestations! The knowledge, the understanding, the comprehending, then *necessitated* the entering in because it partook of that which *was* in manifestation; and thus the *perfect* body, the celestial body, became an earthly body and thus put on flesh. (The explanation to some becomes worse than the first!) This, then: (This has nothing to do with Knowledge, or it is too much knowledge for some of you, for you'll stumble over it; but you asked for it and here it is!)

When the earth became a dwelling place for matter, when gases formed into those things than man sees in nature and in activity about him, then matter began its ascent in the various forms of physical evolution . . . in the *mind* [and Mind, remember, is a synonym for the first-begotten Son] of God! The spirit [as Amilius, the Son] chose to enter (celestial, not an earth spirit—he [Adam] hadn't come into the earth yet!), chose to put on, to become a part of, that which was as a command *not* to be done!

Then those so entering *must* continue through the earth until the body-mind is made perfect for the soul, or the body-celestial again. (262–99)

It is hard to imagine a more explicit, a more beautifully instructive, summary of the origins of the present human condition and its ultimate solution than is contained in those few paragraphs. They embrace a whole philosophy that some might spend a lifetime seeking, and never find. For herein we learn a marvelous secret: we learn from whence we came, and whither we must go. And it is in words such as these that one comes to realize what a remarkable contribution to mankind, albeit little recognized as yet, was made by the late Edgar Cayce. A man of relatively little formal education, and seemingly beset with as many human frailties as the rest of us, his psychic genius set him apart—this, and a great singleness of purpose. His sole objective in life was service to man and God. There have not been many who could match his selfless contribution.

But back to our story . . .

Unfortunately, there are not many substantive clues in the readings from which we can sniff out a reliable approximation as to just when the first influx of souls occurred, back in the ancient annals of prehistoric time. Yet there is at least one—and, happily, it is a rather good one. It is to be found in Reading 2665-2. In that life reading, a very early incarnation is given, preceding [2665]'s Atlantean appearance during the first of the eruptions that ultimately destroyed that fabled continent. We are told that she was among the first peoples to separate into groups, or families. The reading tells of a cave in the ancient and arid plateau region of the American Southwest—once a portion of the now-sunken continent of Lemuria, according to legend, and one of the few early landscapes of the planet that has somehow survived innumerable cataclysmic changes down through the aeons. In that cave, said the reading, drawings then made by the entity may still be seen. And it then added, in startling fashion: "Some ten million years ago"!

No earlier date, to my knowledge, can be found anywhere in the readings on which to pin our ancient origins.[1] Moreover, lest some might be tempted to conclude that a cave-dwelling entity could not have been one of the original thought-form projections of soul-beings in that initial influx with Amilius but must have been one of the "daughters of men" resulting from the later entanglements of the sons and daughters of God in the ways of the flesh, we find such understandable skepticism refuted in Reading 364-12. Therein it states that those from the first influx of souls "became dwellers in the rock, in the caves," or made their homes, "or nests, as it were, in the trees."

Let us move on.

Our next "fix" on the anthropological clock happens to pertain to a former thought-form entity, now know as Mr. [877], who was told that his earliest relationships with his friend Edgar Cayce had occurred during an earthly sojourn that "was nearer to fifty or five hundred thousand years before we even have the beginning of the LAW *as* the Law of One [in Atlantis] manifested!" (877-26).

That's going back pretty far, admittedly, despite the extremely wide latitude in the two given dates. But how far is "pretty far"? For we simply don't know when the teaching of the Law of One had its beginnings in Atlantis. But probably this occurred during the rule of Amilius. And there is this revealing reference, in yet another reading, to that rule:

As to the highest point of civilization, this would first have to be determined according to the standard as to which it would be judged—as to whether the highest point was when Amilius ruled with those understandings, as the one that understood the variations, or whether they become man-made, would depend upon whether we are viewing from a spiritual standpoint or upon that as a purely material or commercial standpoint; for the variations, as we find, extend over a period of some two hundred thousand years. (364-4)

The reading adds that this is a reference to "light years," and elsewhere it is explained that this should not be confused with the current scientific term, in the lexicon of astronomy, that applies to the speed at which light travels through the universe but to "the sun goes down and the sun goes down" years—a phrase, quite frankly, that implies synonymity with our present measurement of the solar year. But we need to consider the possibility—nay, the probability—that the passage of the aeons has seen an appreciable slowdown in the earth's rotation, both axial and orbital.

Finally, from a more esoteric perspective, I think we can justifiably posit that, though the earth may be slowing down, thus lengthening our modern-age year in relation to prehistoric times, man himself has experienced just the reverse: in short, his life span has shrunk in relation to the millennial-like life span of Adam and his early progeny as recorded in Genesis; the life span of the early Atlanteans and their progenitors may well have been comparatively "ageless." Thus, time is relative, and a million years, in the earth's early beginnings, may be equivalent in certain significant respects to a mere thousand in the present.

The Atlantean rule of Amilius, like the much, much later decision of the early Israelites to abandon their God-given rights of self-rule and appoint a king to govern them, may have arisen out of a similar tribal weakness and lack of self-discipline as the original thought-form projections found themselves increasingly out of touch with their spiritual origins and more and more given to fleshly entanglements and the ways of selfishness in the earth-plane.

The separation of the sexes had already begun, and this, of itself, was not necessarily counted as a sin as long as the androgynous god-beings in the separation into paired companions (like Amilius and Lilith) retained their essential purity and did not lust after the flesh-forms in the earth. (For as Reading 275–36 put it, though they were thought-forms, *"they had a body!"* But either it was a body-celestial or it was rapidly on its way to becoming an earth-body, trapping the soul-entity in its material encasement through the downward-gravitating desires of the mind-body of the entity.)

Eventually this led to the need to reawaken the drifting souls to the awareness of their spiritual heritage, now half-forgotten. Amilius, as the Elder Brother of all the other souls, and that one initially responsible for their predicament, apparently decided to take personal control of a deteriorating situation. Thus, His long rule began, and under that rule, the Law of One was presumably established. Those who adhered to the Law, based on Amilius's teachings, became known as the children of Light, and in their temples of service they sought to draw the wavering sons and daughters of God back from the brink of total separation and darkness. However, those who succumbed to the ways of selfishness, and further separation from the Light, became identified eventually as the sons of Belial—an expression signifying lawlessness. Their rebellious ruler was the Prince of Darkness, whose domain was in the earth-plane. The forces of Darkness thereafter waged constant battle with the spiritual rule of the Light, Mind, the Word, embodied in Amilius.

Here, as it were, we encounter the prelude to that turbulent phase in Atlantean history, showing Amilius's growing perception of the problem:

In the period, then—some hundred, some ninety-eight thousand years before the entry of Ram into India—there lived in this land of Atlantis one Amilius, who had first noted . . . the separations of the beings as inhabited that portion of the earth's sphere or individuals. As to their forms in the physical sense, these were much rather of the nature of thought-forms, or able to push out of themselves in that direction in which its development took shape in thought—much in the way and manner as the amoeba would in the waters of a stagnant bay, or lake, in the present. As these took form, by the gratifying of their own desire for that as builded or added to the material conditions, they became hardened or set—much in the form of the existent human body of the [present] day, with that of color as partook of its surroundings much in the manner as the chameleon in the present. Hence coming into that form as the red, or the mixture peoples—or colors; known then later by the associations as the red race. (364-3)

Yet, to comprehend the growing evil in their midst, we need to examine certain other passages that reveal the extent to which some of the more wayward entities were abusing their abilities to call upon the Creative Forces for the fulfillment of their desires in any direction:

These, then, are the manners in which the entities, those beings, those souls, in the beginning partook of, or developed. Some brought about monstrosities, as those of its (that entity's) association by its projection with its association with beasts of various characters. Hence those of the Styx, satyr, and the like; those of the sea, or mermaid; those of the unicorn, and those of the various forms. (364-10)

In Atlantean land during those periods when there were the divisions between those of the Law of One and the sons of Belial, or the offspring of what was the pure race and those who had projected themselves into creatures that become "the sons of men" (as the terminology would be) rather than the creatures of God. (1416-1)

The other group—those who followed the Law of One—had a standard. The sons of Belial had no standard, save of self, self-aggrandizement.

Those entities [termed "things"] that were then the producers (as we would term today), or the laborers, the farmers or the artisans, or those who were in the positions of what we call in the present just machines, were those that were projections of the individual activity of the group [known as sons of Belial].

And it was over these, then, and the relationships that they bore to those that were in authority, that the differences arose. (877-26)

Ah, yes. Differences indeed! Those same differences found their karmic echo, perhaps, in the slave-owning era of our own land, when a privileged class sought to suppress the human rights of others for their own material gain. They lost.

But let us revert to that earlier reference to "the entry of Ram into India." It may provide us with yet another clue to the ancient ticking of time on our anthropological clock.

Ram, or Rama, was one of the first of the great initiates, and he was the founder of the Vedic teachings. (Literally, *ram* means "the leader of the peaceful flock.") Rama's period in history is uncertain; some have estimated 5,000 B.C. or perhaps even earlier. But let us take the given date. Reading 364–3 tells us that Amilius's reign in Atlantis apparently began about one hundred thousand years before the days of Rama in India. Or more precisely, some ninety-eight thousand years ahead of the latter. So, there we are: 103,000 B.C. Take it or leave it, as you wish.

On with our story!

Despite the efforts of the children of the Law of One, the Atlantean race and culture seemed doomed to eventual self-extinction through the increasingly destructive activities of the sons of Belial. Great technological advancements, which had gradually supplanted the declining spiritual power of the race, only led to worse abuses. First, there was the mighty crystal, whose prisms could gather and harness the incredible energies in the rays from far-off Arcturus or the sun of our own little solar system; originally under the direct control of the priests and priestesses of the Law of One, that control was gradually subverted by the sons of Belial, leading to the first of several great eruptions that proved to be the eventual undoing of Atlantis. Lasers and other destructive forces were also unleashed; and as given in Reading 195–29, "That thrown off will be returned"—not necessarily in the same form but with a similar degree of destructiveness, for that is a spiritual law. Yet the wayward Atlanteans paid scant heed to *any* law. The first of the eruptions, breaking up the proud continent into a series of islands, did not deter those who acknowledged no power but their own. Nor did the second cataclysmic upheaval serve to chastise them.

And so the realization came to Amilius that a "second creation" would be necessary, bringing into the earth a flesh-form man, but of pure origins, who would arise from the impending ruins of Atlantis and propagate himself from his own kind, repopulating and replenishing the flood- and earthquake-ravaged planet over which he would be given dominion. His name would be Adam, or *adama,* meaning "the red earth."

As a prelude to Adamic man's appearance, however, there were to be forerunners who would prepare the way. For "preparations were made," it says of that advance era in Reading 3579–1, "for the advent of the souls of men to be brought to their relationship with God." (A similar cycle of preparation, in fact, exists today, if Cayce was right, as we await the advent of a new age and a new race in the earth, and Reading 5749–5 indicates that Edgar Cayce himself entered as a "forerunner" of the approaching new order. We shall shortly see that he was apparently repeating his ancient role in a similar capacity.)

To continue:

The second influx of souls, under the direction of Amilius, began with those chosen to be forerunners. Androgynous beings, even as the soul-entities in the first influx had been, they nevertheless differed from their ancient predecessors (of whom some were themselves, in fact, now returning) by being "flesh-form" entities. From their number, in time, the very purest daughters would presumably be selected as the channels for the initial projection by Amilius of the five racial groupings of Adamic man, the five colors, the five primal nations, that would become known historically as the forebears of modern man—in brief, ourselves.

One among those forerunners of the second creation, however, was to have a special role to play. Now that Amilius, the Maker, would no longer be able to commune directly with those flesh-beings projected by himself (for as the soul-entities took on flesh-form, His higher vibrational rate would automatically separate Him from their three-dimensional view), He recognized the need for a representative in the earth at that time. Such a representative, though also a flesh-form, would adhere to the Law, counseling men everywhere in the ways of peace and brotherhood, as opposed to more disruptive and violent solutions to their problems. It was all a part of the Divine Plan emerging, so that the coming Adamic Age could be safely ushered-in.

And so, Asapha entered. We shall meet him in the next chapter.

Meanwhile, Amilius foresaw yet another necessity in His unfolding plan for the eventual salvation of mankind. It involved an act of enormous Self-sacrifice. Yet He never wavered.

He now realized that He himself would have to enter into one of the five proposed prototypes for the new, flesh-form race, and He chose to come as Adam, the Son of man, entering His own creation a second time but now as a *fleshly* projection of Himself, Amilius, the "Upper Adam." Though androgynous and without earthly father or mother, He would be a mortal, and subject to mortal limitations. In this way, He—Mind, Light, the Word— would become a flesh-form Pattern for all of the souls trapped in the earth, as He led them through a cycle of numerous incarnations, slowly and painstakingly, out of the self-imposed prison of their earthly vibrations and back to their original, unfallen estate as One with Him, in the celestial body and the heavenly realm.

It has been said that we are His brethren, *His individual selves*— men in the earth, but gods in the making. And where does the evolving soul go when fully developed? Back to its Maker, as a cell reborn in the Body of God:

And ye must be one—one with another, one with Him—if ye would be, as indeed ye are—corpuscles in the *life flow* of thy Redeemer! (1391-1)

4. When the Two Were as One

In the beginning, there was presented that that became as the Sons of God, in that male and female were as in one.
—*Edgar Cayce Reading* 364–7

Jesus said: On the day when you were one, you became two.
—*The Gospel According to Thomas* (Logion 11)

THE COUNCIL OF FORTY-FOUR
(Asapha and Affa; Egypt, 50,722 B.C.)

In February 1925, Edgar Cayce obtained a follow-up life reading for himself.

As often turned out to be the case with such follow-up readings, whether for himself or others, there were surprising new disclosures in this one. It was as if the spiritual progress made by an entity in using the information in a former reading to further its soul development determined its degree of readiness to learn more about its past lives. And in knowing more about its past, and the fruits thereof, the earnest seeker after truth would obviously be that much better equipped to shape the course of its future. For all our yesterdays are a collective image of what we are today, and the living present, with its opportunities, is like a sharp sculptor's chisel with which we may change the shape of the image, modifying the shadow it will cast upon our tomorrows. The good in our past should be an incentive to new achievements; whereas the flaws, if seen and acknowledged, can be erased and the marble restructured to a more perfect likeness of our ideal.

In Edgar's case, with that particular reading, the revealing new information was of a mixed nature. He learned more about a downward-gravitating cycle in the earth, during the Trojan wars, that adversely affected his ability in the present to control his wrath or displeasure in certain situations. But he was greatly encouraged to learn of a very early incarnation that had been omitted from his initial life reading. It fitted between his initial entry in the beginning, with Amilius, as one of the sons of God in that first influx of souls and his memorable Egyptian cycle as the priestly Ra Ta, who had journeyed under a psychic compulsion to that sunlit region of the world from his adoptive homeland on the slopes of Mount Ararat to fulfill a unique destiny.

Now he discovered that he had come as a forerunner in the *second* influx of souls, "when the forces in flesh came to dwell in the earth's plane." The reading continued:

The entity was *among the first* to inhabit the earth *in that form,* and was from the beginning in the earth's forces. In this we find the larger development in the entity, for then [the soul was] able to contain in the Oneness of the forces as given in the sons of men, and realizing the Fatherhood of the Creator.

In the present plane we find that ever urge to be drawn nearer to the spiritual elements of every force. Hence, in the summing up and use of these, let the entity keep the spiritual forces ever magnified, in action, deed, and in truth, For, in earth's plane, every element of the physical or mental, or spiritual nature, is judged by the relation to spiritual force. (294–19; italics added)

And there the matter rested. The reading included no elaboration as to Edgar's identity or purpose in that first flesh-form incarnation. However, the reference to "the larger development in the entity" in its ability "to contain in the Oneness of the forces as given in the sons of men, and realizing the Fatherhood of the Creator" provided a clue of sorts: One could infer from such a laudatory reference that it had been a notable incarnation, probably affecting the lives of many. The spiritual lessons gained and applied must have been significant, in fact, since their influence upon Cayce in the present was given as "that ever urge to be drawn nearer to the spiritual elements of every force."

A few months later, a seemingly unrelated series of readings was given while Cayce was still residing in Dayton, Ohio, before the oft-urged move to Virginia Beach. Those readings, known today as the "5748" series, were primarily concerned with an ancient gathering of forty-four world leaders among the sons of men to discuss ways and means of ridding the planet of fearsome beasts then overrunning the earth in certain areas.

Based on a very precise date of 50,722 B.C., as supplied some years later in one of the Search for God readings (namely, 262–39, given in February 1933 at Virginia Beach), that urgent conclave must have occurred after Amilius's departure from the Atlantean scene; for the five nations of early mankind were now in their formative stages and already being inhabited and ruled by the sons of men. Also, by our calculations, it was a period some thirty-nine thousand years before Adam's advent during the next return of the Age of Virgo, which marked the commencement of our present Grand Cycle of the Ages. Finally, it preceded Cayce's Egyptian incarnation as Ra Ta by about forty thousand years. (Actually, a highly questionable and most unlikely dating for the great conclave had been supplied in one of the original Dayton readings, 5748–2, suggesting a time frame of some ten-and-a-half million years ago! But Hugh Lynn had properly sensed that this date was flawed, reflecting a sudden malfunction in Edgar's psychic calculator, and it was he who made the inquiry resulting in the corrected dating, 50,722 B.C., given eight years later. For it was obvious to him, as it must be to any astute researcher, that the period covered by the particular readings in question concerned the *second* influx of souls, not the first.)

If anything emerges with certainty from the Edgar Cayce readings, it is the incontrovertible fact that great events on the stage of human history, as well as in the realm of so-called natural phenomena, tend to occur in a cyclical pattern. Scientists, too, have observed this fact to some extent, without being able to explain it. Thus, when I pored over the details in the 5748 series and began analyzing the teachings and activities of that early Egyptian leader who had drawn together the forty-four world representatives of his day, seeking a peaceful rather than a destructive solution to the dilemma then facing mankind, the parallels with the later Ra Ta cycle—occurring in essentially the same environment —were stunning. For one thing, both were primarily active in the "second rule" of their respective epochs, although the one—Asapha—came as the ruler, whereas the other—Ra Ta—appeared as a spiritual leader, though with a ruler's supreme authority in his final years. Their teachings were based on essentially the same spiritual precepts, supporting the universal laws. Both were peacemakers. And, finally, both appeared on the world scene at identical times of crisis, using their spiritual powers of persuasion to rally all other world leaders under a common banner, re-establishing unity of purpose through the Law of Oneness: "The Lord thy God is One!"

Implicit in these parallels, of course, was the obvious likelihood that the Ra Ta era in Egypt was simply a "repeat" cycle, with appropriate variations, of the great spiritual accomplishments in that earlier Egyptian epoch, when a priestlike ruler, named Asapha, had assembled the Council of Forty-four. Thus, given the workings of mass karma at a planetary level, what more logical deduction could one make than to conclude that the selfsame entity had led both cycles? He who had ruled in the earlier Egyptian cycle had returned to the familiar scene, impelled by the same spiritual forces set in motion by Amilius on both occasions, to take a directing role in the spiritual affairs of the planet in what was to be a permanent closing of the Atlantean epoch and a critical developmental phase in the infant Adamic Age under way in the days of Ra Ta.

Yet another intriguing aspect of the Ra Ta cycle, linking it by spiritual roots to the earlier, under Asapha, was the fact that the priestly Ra Ta had purportedly received psychic guidance from the beginning, compelling him to lead King Ararat and his people out of their mountainous homeland into Egypt. Why Egypt? Many reasons, as we shall later see. But one was undoubtedly an answering chord from within, from that earlier cycle, if our speculation is sound. Additionally, compelled by one knows not what atavistic promptings, Ra Ta had conducted archaeological research in a portion of the Sahara where he had presumably reigned some forty thousand years earlier as Asapha. In the Ra Ta diggings, the site of a large colony of so-called things, bearing tail-like protuberances, was uncovered. Ra's research established that they had been sun worshipers, even as those natives in his own day, and that they had apparently migrated to the Sahara region many thousands of years earlier to escape persecution at the hands of the sons of Belial, who had treated them as automatons. It was presumably in their new land, coming under Asapha's benign rule, that they became sun worshipers, envisioning their new king, or pharaoh, as the incarnate Sun-god. (The historical parallels are stunningly obvious. It is like a tune replayed, with only the octaves altered.)

Finally, in confirming the cyclical pattern of history, there is a much more modern parallel, which I am somewhat reluctant to commit to writing, though its time has surely come. It is a story, I am told, with no documentation to support it. Nevertheless, it was related to me by Gladys Davis Turner, Edgar Cayce's longtime secretary and a virtual member of the Cayce household after her initial employment in 1923. It pertains to an incident in Edgar's psychic career that predated her arrival on the scene, of course, since it concerned Woodrow Wilson's vision of a League of Nations and its dramatic impact upon the Paris peace conference in 1919. The readings say of Wilson's ill-starred efforts that the Christ himself sat at the peace table, in the presence of that very sincere and humble president of the United States. What is not mentioned in any of the readings, however, is the "background" story; I relate it here.

During World War I, Gladys explained, David Kahn—a close friend and lifelong spokesman of Cayce's—became associated with two first cousins of Woodrow Wilson. Through that association, arrangements were made for Edgar Cayce to come to Washington and give a "very private" reading for President Wilson in connection with the proposed peace plans. The whole affair was treated with absolute confidentiality, and Mr. Cayce was not even permitted to be accompanied by a recording secretary. But it is believed that Wilson's famous Fourteen Points may have emerged—perhaps verbatim—from that Cayce reading. Failure of the other Allies to accept Wilson's idealistic proposals, and subsequent senatorial opposition, reportedly broke Wilson's heart, though he was awarded the Nobel Peace Prize in 1920. If ours is an accurate account, the League of Nations concept originated, in part, with Cayce, who, much earlier, as a representative of Amilius in the earth, had twice before attempted to bind the nations of the world together in peaceful cooperation in his two Egyptian cycles; as Uhjltd, the nomadic Persian ruler whose appearance followed Cayce's Egyptian incarnations, his activities had been along much the same lines. (History does indeed seem to repeat itself, but more particularly so if the same soul-entity is allowed to reincarnate with a new opportunity to play out a variation of its former role under fresh circumstances that favor its efforts.)

As a recent postscript to Wilson's tragic failure, I found these words by Haynes Johnson, in the June 26, 1983, edition of the *Washington Post,* strangely moving: "It is said that when Woodrow Wilson went to France at the end of World War I, everywhere expressing his dream of a League of Nations that would banish war from the Earth, the millions who turned out to cheer him did so with an emotional fervor that was frightening in its intensity and spontaneity. Reporters who accompanied him wondered whether even a Caesar or Napoleon had ever stirred such an emotional outpouring from the masses."

(Indeed! Or a *Christ?* . . .)

If our narrative seems to have strayed somewhat off course in its pursuit of parallels, the purpose of such a diversion will now become plain. Actually, it has led us full circle, back to our starting point. For we find that the first reference, by name, to Asapha (or to Affa, as his companionate soul, or female counterpart, in the androgynous flesh-body of that particular incarnation) occurred in a reading that dealt with the Christ appearing down through the ages as a living Presence in the hearts of certain individuals deemed worthy of carrying on His work in the earth-plane. The reading indicated that this had been an observable pattern in human history ever since the Master's initial entry as Amilius, in the beginning. Then, in a passage that quite plainly identifies Asapha as that Egyptian leader who convened the Council of Forty-four, we read: "He [the Christ, Amilius] has walked and talked with men as in those days as [of] Asapha, or Affa, in those periods when those of the same Egyptian land were giving those counsels to the many nations [an obvious allusion to the Council of Forty-four], when there would be those saving of the physical from that of their own making in the physical" (364–8).

The karmic consequences implicit in the above reference to the "saving of the physical from that of their own making in the physical" is worth noting. Later, we shall see how Asapha sought to invoke aid from the Divine Forces in meeting the threat to mankind from the beasts overrunning the planet rather than re- sorting to violent solutions that would obviously perpetuate the karmic cycle.

Before proceeding with other details of the story, we must pause to consider a second reference to Asapha, in a reading given scarcely a week after the reading just cited, in April 1932. This time, it was disclosed that Cayce's Persian incarnation as Uhjltd, the nomadic ruler, had followed *two* early Egyptian incarnations, one as Asapha and the other as the priest Ra Ta. Somewhat curi- ously, though, the reading assigns an alternate name to Ra Ta, "Adonis." Yet I found this easily clarified with a bit of research. Gaskell identifies Adonis as a symbol of the Higher Self—the in- carnate God born in the soul. "Adonis," he continues, "was con- ceived of the Divine Father and born of Myrrha—the purified lower nature." (How closely this parallels the account given in the readings of Ra Ta's entry through a daughter of Zu, but without earthly father!) Gaskell continues: "The incarnate God is therefore bound by the Divine law of the reincarnating cycle, and has to pass through short periods of earth life or physical existence, with intermediate periods of astral and mental existence of longer dura- tion" until the soul is made perfect. Gaskell then cites Hippolytus: " 'Now the Assyrians call this [mystery of soul development] Adonis (or Endymion).' "[1] These mythological trappings, of course, should not be misconstrued to suggest that Edgar Cayce, as

Ra Ta, was a soul-entity any more godlike than the rest of us. In fact, a Cayce reading on the Ra Ta epoch is careful to lay to rest any such misconception, based on Ra Ta's unusual birth and appearance, as well as that he was later worshiped as the Sun-god by the native Egyptians: "Ye say, then, that such an entity was a god! No. No—ye only say that because there is the misunderstanding of what were the characters or types of spiritual evolution as related to *physical* evolution in the earth at that period" (281–42).

Here is the specific quotation on Cayce's two Egyptian incarnations, first as Asapha and later as the priestly Ra Ta (or "Adonis"), preceding his Persian experience:

In the first, we find that the entity Uhjltd [Cayce] was an incarnation of Asapha and also of the priest [Ra Ta], both experiences being in Egypt— or Adonis and Asapha. In entering, then, we find, in the land then known as Iran [Aryan land?], there were those that had held true to those teachings that had been propounded by the teachers [note plural] in the Egyptian. (294–142)

Meanwhile, picking up again the main thread of our story, it is time to review some of the highlights of that Council of Forty-four in the days of Asapha and his companionate entity, Affa.

We find, to begin with, that "the first ruler of groups" in those days when the five nations were in their formative stages had established himself "in that place in the upper Nile, near what is now known as the Valley of Tombs" (5748–1). He was succeeded by Asapha, whose authority apparently extended beyond his own immediate realm, since it was he who determined the rulership in the other tribal spheres of the planet where emergent mankind was gathered together for its own protection and evolutionary development. In addition to the Sahara and the Nile region, under Asapha's personal rule, this included Tibet, Mongolia, Caucasia, and what is now Norway; also the southern Cordillera and Peru; and those plateau regions now known as Utah, Arizona, and New Mexico. As for the portions of Atlantis still intact, most notably Poseidia, these were not mentioned, presumably because their inhabitants held themselves aloof at that time from the more "primitive" sons of men and their problems. Moreover, the beasts that terrorized other portions of the planet may have been of no direct concern to the Atlanteans, who had long since eliminated them from their broken lands.

Asapha's approach to the problem, resulting in the convening of the Council of Forty-four, was expressed in this manner:

In the second rule [headed by Asapha] there came peace and quietude to the peoples, through the manner of the ruler's power over the then known world forces. At that period, man exchanged with the forces in each sphere that necessary for the propagation of the peoples of the sphere then occupied. In each of the spheres given was the rule set under some individual by this second rule [i.e., Asapha's] in now Egyptian country, and the period when the mind of that ruler brought to self, through the compliance with those Universal Laws ever existent, then that ruler set about to gather those wise men from the various groups to compile those as that ruler felt the necessary understanding to all peoples for the indwelling of the Divine Forces to become understood and to break away from the fear of the animal kingdom then overrunning the earth. (5748–1)

The next reading in the series pointed out that the number of souls then in the earth-plane was 133,000,000. Asapha's rule lasted 199 years. It was in his twenty-eighth year that he "began to gather the peoples together" to study the grave situation confronting them, "surrounding himself with those of that [Egyptian] land and of the various lands wherein the *human* life dwelled at that period. The numbers of the people that came together for the purpose then numbering some forty and four [44]" (5748–2; italics added).

In the next reading on the subject, we have this interesting observation by the sleeping Cayce:

Then, we have the gathering together then of this group, from the farthest places—forty and four [44]. As we see, this number will run through many numbers, for, as we find there is the law pertaining to each and every element significant to man's existence considered and given in one manner or form by the groups as gathered at this meeting. (5748–3)

Whatever its significance here, students of numerology will note that 44 is one of the four so-called master numbers, which retain their given value; the other three are 11, 22, and 33. Let the interested reader pursue that arcane matter further if it appeals to his or her mystical sense. But we will leave it at this juncture to continue the thread of our narrative.

Asapha's advice to the council was to avoid the use of warlike or destructive measures to cope with the murderous beasts that threatened their existence. It was hard advice, and many members of the council apparently demurred. It offended them. They felt a need for swift and violent action. Yet Asapha held firm to spiritual principles:

And the first as was given by the ruler was, then, that the force that gives man, in his weak state, as it were, the ability to subdue and overcome the great beasts that inhabit the plane of man's existence must come from a higher source. (5748-3)

After many moons of debate, the wisdom of Asapha's counsel was demonstrated in a startling manner, as the hand of God resolved their dilemma for them in an unexpected fashion. We find an account of what happened contained in this excerpt from a reading for Mr. [5249], who was told that he had been one of the forty-four council members at that memorable conclave in the tents of a prehistoric time:

The entity then was among those [forty-four] who were of that group gathered to rid the earth of the enormous animals which overran the earth, but ice, the entity found, nature, God, changed the poles and the animals were destroyed, though man attempted it in that activity of the meetings. (5249-1)

If Cayce was right, a similar shifting of the poles will occur at the close of the present century and the dawning of the next. It will signal the dayspring of the Aquarian Age and the fifth root race. It will also follow closely on the heels of yet another prophesied event, which Cayce predicted would occur in 1998: the Second Coming of the Lord. What changes may we expect to see take place upon our planet in the wake of such a wondrous synchronicity of major events?

AGE OF VIRGO
(Aczine and Asule; Atlantis, 12,800 B.C.)

In one of her life readings, the entity [288], who had incarnated in the late Atlantean epoch as a ruler in Poseidia named Asule, asked an interesting question and received an interesting answer:

Q–1. *In Atlantis, was I associated with Amilius? If so, how?*
A–1. One as projected by that entity as to a ruler or *guide* for many, with its associating entity [294, Edgar Cayce]. (288–29)

The date of that androgynous incarnation had been given as 12,800 B.C. in an earlier life reading for [288] that explored her past associations with [294], or Edgar Cayce, who had been her twin soul in the beginning:

We find these [two], as in the present earth's plane, have had many experiences together, and their soul and spirit are well knit, and must of necessity present each that they may be one. For we find *in the beginning* that they, these two (which we shall speak of as "they" until separated), were as one in mind, soul, spirit, body; and in the first earth's plane as the voice over many waters, when the glory of the Father's giving of the earth's indwelling of man was both male and female in one. (288–6; italics added)

But whereas the male aspect had apparently been dominant in the initial projection as a thought-form being, during that first influx of souls, as well as in the days of Asapha and Affa in Egypt, now the female counterpart took the ascendant role in this late-Atlantean flesh-form appearance in Poseidia:

In *flesh-form* in earth's plane we find the first [if we omit the male rule of Asapha] in that of the Poseidian forces, when both were confined in the body of the female; for this being the stronger in the then expressed or applied forces found manifestations for each in that form. . . . The experiences there were as these: These two were [involved in] the giving of the spiritual development in the land [Atlantis], and the giving of the uplift to the peoples of the day and age.

In 12,800 B.C. we find together. . . . The desire remained in the One, for which the Oneness was created. (288–6; italics added)

The first reference to a given name for the androgynous flesh-being in the Poseidian rule was "Aczine":

Q–1. *Will you please give us the names of the personalities?*
A–1. We have given the personalities. The names of individuals as were in the earth's plane, in the first (Poseidia) that of Aczine. (288–10)

Curiously, though, all subsequent references to that Poseidian incarnation in [288]'s life readings give her name as "Asule." On this basis, it seems to be a reasonable speculation that the name Aczine, which Cayce had given originally, applied to his own identity as the companionate soul.

This late Atlantean incarnation took place in the Age of Virgo— a time, by our calculations, when Amilius implemented His plan to project into the earth as the Son of man, or Adam, appearing as an androgynous flesh-being in the fabulous Garden of Eden. (Reading 364–4 describes the lost Atlantis as "this, the Eden of the world," so we may assume that Adam's earthly paradise was somewhere within that realm, or what then remained of it.) But after the separation of Adam's companionate self, or twin soul, Eve, sin eventually entered. They were driven from the garden. Eastward they fled, where, of the five racial forms of the new root race then emerging, they became the progenitors of the red in its final condition as flesh-form man.

Sin entered, too, in the fair city of Alta, where Asule, with her companionate soul, Aczine, reigned over the Poseidians, lending much assistance to the common people of that day. Apparently Asule was one of the few remaining androgynes in Atlantis during that period of its last flickerings of glory preceding its final demise. The date, by our estimation, was perhaps half a millennium before Adam's appearance in the land. Many, the readings indicate, were envious of Asule's androgynous state and her spiritual powers of projection, reminiscent of the activities of the sons and daughters of God in a former era. In an age of flesh-beings, her status was unique, and it bespoke the spiritual purpose of her rule in a land where the sons of Belial had not ceased to work their mischief. Observing their ways, Asule eventually yielded to certain temptations. With the desire no longer remaining "in the One, for which the Oneness was created," the entity [288] sought carnal gratification "with one of lower estate"—an animal-like being, or "thing," presumably, brutish in its passions—"and through this treachery of one not capable of understanding, it brought physical defects in the limbs of these [companion souls] then contained in the one body in physical form." A comatose state resulted, with "karma exercised in coma," and "there was brought the separation," or the entering into the land of the Unknown (288–6).

It is a story with obvious parallels to Adam's "fall," in that same general epoch heralding the birth of humankind. Thus, not inappropriately, Asule's fateful choice can be expressed in the same biblical terms applicable to Adam's, a bit later on: "As given in the injunction from the Maker: 'I have this day set before you good and evil. Choose the light or the darkness' "(288–6).

That fateful incarnation marked the last androgynous appearance of [288] and [294]. Indeed, the androgynous state apparently terminated permanently with Adam's advent, not to be resumed until man could put off the flesh and regain the body-celestial. Yet, in examining their subsequent entries into the earth-plane as separate entities, both [288] and her companionate soul seem to have tried in their varied incarnations (we shall take note, along the way, of [294]'s exceptions) to re-establish, not only for themselves but for the rest of fallen mankind, a condition of oneness with the Maker:

At present we find they are again together, still in different divisions, positions or circumstances, each paying out that which has been gained or merited. . . . In this [present experience] they are again united in soul and in spirit force, and through the joy and the pleasure of selfless service they may again know the meaning of these as given.

They need only remain in the future faithful one to the other, ever giving, ever retaining those joys of the relations that bring and give of self in service to others; and these bring joy, peace, and again uniting of body, soul, and spirit in the next [a reference to Cayce's prophesied return in 1998?]. Remain faithful, therefore, unto the end; gaining those joys through daily acts of selflessness for and with others, remembering that in these manifestations they (and all souls) become knit one with the other. (288–6)

As for Adam, his sin opened his eyes:

Q–3.   When did the knowledge come to Jesus that He was to be the Savior of the world?
A–3.   When He fell in Eden. (2067–7)

A surprising glimpse of the paradisiacal garden is provided, incidentally, in the following excerpt from one of the readings, which tells us that Adam and Eve were not altogether "alone." They had other visitors and "watchers" than the serpent, and perhaps other temptations than the apple:

. . . *the garden called Eden.* There we find the entity was among those who looked on the activity of the mother of mankind. The entity was among "the things" and yet was touched in person . . . in heart . . . and sought to know the meaning . . . for it saw then the fruit, the leaves, trees, which had their spiritual meanings in people's lives. (5373–1)

What, precisely, was the sin of Adam? Was it carnal knowledge of Eve? or cohabitation with "one of lower estate," as Asule's sin had been? We are reluctant to speculate. Yet a definition of the "original sin" was given in Reading 262–125: *willful disobedience.* That is knowledge enough for our purposes. And its corollary, arising from guilt, is the initial impulse to blame another: "The *woman* Thou gavest me, *she* persuaded me and I did eat!" (262–125).

Finally, here is a philosophical summary of the matter, which the reader may enjoy wrestling with:

Adam . . . first discerned that *from himself,* not of the beasts about him, could be drawn—was drawn—that which made for the propagation of beings in the flesh, that made for that companionship as seen by creation in the material worlds about same. The story, the tale (if chosen to be called such), is one and the same. The apple, as "the apple of the eye," the desire of that companionship innate in that created, as innate in the Creator, that brought companionship into creation itself. *Get that one!* (364–5; italics added)

After giving us that walnut to crack, just for openers, the next paragraph of the reading cuts into the core of the apple:

In this there comes, then, that which is set before that created—or having taken on that form, [capable of] projecting itself in whatever direction it chose to take, . . . for were He not the Son of the living God made manifest, that He might be the companion in a made world, in material manifested things, with the injunction to subdue all, being all in the material things under subjection—by that ability to project itself in its way? knowing itself, as given, to be a portion of the whole, in, through, of, by the whole? In this desire, then, keep—as the injunction was—thine self separate; *of* that seen, but *not* that seen. The apple, then, that desire for that which made for the associations that bring carnal-minded influences of that brought as sex influence, known in a material world, and the partaking of same is that which brought the influence in the lives of that in the symbol of the serpent, that made for that which creates the desire that may be only satisfied in gratification of carnal forces, as partake of the world and its influences about same—rather than of the spiritual emanations from which it has its source. Will control—[or] inability of will control, if we may put it in common parlance. (364–5; italics added)

The Adam in us all, Cayce seems to imply, must be overcome by the Christ within us.

This does *not* rule out the use of the procreative function, however, as two souls come together in oneness and purity of purpose. This function, as a natural consequence of the human condition as it came to exist after Adam, was properly defined in one of [288]'s readings, respecting her love match with Uhjltd in the Persian incarnation, as the giving of self to "the sex desire between the two for the developing" toward the spiritual ideal of oneness, in the act of procreation; for "in that we find it counted as righteousness in both" (288–6). The outcome of that particular union, as we shall find explained more fully in a later chapter, was a son named Zend, who was an incarnation of the Master and a man of peace and virtue—the evolving Christ, who had been the fallen Adam. It was at once a blessing and an absolution for all concerned.

Each Grand Cycle of the Ages, lasting some 25,920 years, marks the precession of the equinoxes through the twelve signs of the celestial zodiac. Because it is a backward-moving passage, following the earth's polar wobble in its infinitely slow gyrations, the Great Year cycle begins with Pisces and ends with Aries. This, of course, is just the reverse of the Sun's annual orbit through the twelve heavenly signs from Aries to Pisces.

At present, we are about to complete the 2,160-year backward passage through the Age of Pisces, the sign of the Fishes; and we straddle the cusp of the coming Age of Aquarius, the sign of the Man. By traditional calculation, assuming that the Piscean Age had its beginnings about 160 B.C., in the days of Hipparchus, the famous Greek astronomer who "rediscovered" the precession of the equinoxes, this means that the current Great Year will not reach its close until A.D. 23,760, as it passes into 0° of the Age of Aries.

But let us take a more esoteric view of the subject, one, I think, that has not previously been explored in its full dimensions. It will undoubtedly upset a lot of applecarts. No matter! Apples are not all that sacred to us: we consider the trouble they brought to man in the beginning. The beginning—that is just where we wish to start; for it is our premise that the advent of Adam occurred in the Age of Virgo, the sign of the Virgin. (On this point, we are not only able to present supportive evidence from the readings, in correlation with the generations of Adam's progeny as recorded in Genesis, but we shall draw on E. W. Bullinger's bold hypothesis, presented almost a century ago to a world then unprepared to receive it, that the original zodiacal map—probably conceived by Adam or Enoch—was really no more nor less than the heavenly pattern of a Man, the seed of a Virgin, who was destined to become a crucified Savior, and eventually return to claim His own.)

And so, if we are to adopt the last Age of Virgo (ca. 13,119 to 10,960 B.C.) as the commencement point for our present Great Year cycle, where will it end? If we are no longer headed full circle back to Aries, as the traditional map of our Great Year journey would have it, where then are we headed? Anyone familiar with the twelve signs of the zodiac and able to trace them in clockwise rotation will easily see that we are headed toward Libra, the sign of the Balance. And interestingly enough, it is the only sign in the zodiac that is not a creaturely sign; it is, rather, a symbol of Judgment.

Prepare yourself for a stunning surprise.

Edgar Cayce, in one of his own life readings that drew on his ancient wisdom as the High Priest Ra, in Egypt, in association with the Master as Hermes, had this to say of mankind's evolutionary destination:

> This building [the Great Pyramid, of which Hermes was the master architect] . . . was formed according to that which had been worked out by Ra Ta in the [Libyan] mount as related to the position of the various stars, that acted in the place about which this particular solar system circles in its activity [a reference to the zodiac], *going towards what?* That same name as to which the priest was banished—*the constellation of Libra,* or to Libya were these people sent. (294–151; italics added)

The mysterious "Hermes," who enters our story in the next chapter, was actually none other than the prophet Enoch, an incarnation of Adam. (Not only do the readings themselves seem to support this interpretation as to His true identity, but it has long been an accepted fact in Islamic tradition and esoteric lore.)

Finally, then: If Cayce foresaw the Age of Libra (ca. A.D. 10,641 to 12,800) as our ultimate destination, does this mean that Adamic man will reach his final fulfillment and spiritual regeneration in that age of judgment? Will the earth, as we know it, exist no more, as a regenerated mankind leaves it permanently behind to ascend heavenward on the etheric current of the universal vibration? These are cogent questions for us. Add another: In glimpsing Libra as the terminal point of our long journey, can it be doubted that Cayce equally knew that Virgo marked our beginnings in the flesh, as Adamic man? We posit the strong likelihood that Cayce, as the exiled priest Ra Ta in the Libyan mount, may have received instruction in the arcana of the zodiac from that great initiate, Hermes, also identified as Enoch, and an incarnation of Adam himself.

This speculation leads us, now, to a consideration of Bullinger's hypothesis, mentioned earlier. It has a most interesting part to play in our unique view of the Virgoan age.

The thrust of Bullinger's theory, presented in an obscure book titled *The Witness of the Stars,*[2] is that the original zodiac, of which our present-day version is a scarcely recognizable copy, was a mystical depiction, drawn in celestial symbols, of an ancient prophecy attributable perhaps to Enoch or even to Adam. That prophecy, of which recognizable echoes are found in various books of the Old Testament, tells of the coming of a Messiah—that Lamb slain from the foundation of the world, a sacrificial offering for the salvation of a lost mankind; the Son of God, born as a man and dying as a man; crucified, and resurrected; a Redeemer, who would return after two thousand years to claim His own.

In Bullinger's presentation, there is also a symbolic relationship between the twelve zodiacal signs and the twelve sons of Jacob, suggesting that Adam, Seth, or Enoch—the supposed originators of the zodiacal legend—had precognition of the entire genesis of Jewish history and the evoluton of the Messiah as that "Branch" out of the stem of Jesse.

Bullinger, a direct descendant of the great Bullinger of the Swiss Reformation, was an Anglican clergyman and a renowned scholar, as well as a formidable linguist. No fanatic or Christian fundamentalist, he backed up his startling hypothesis with a scholar's logic and the true researcher's indefatigable thirst for detail and documentation. Consequently, his book is an impressive *tour de force*. I can only refer the interested reader to that source, for there is not space here to give a full presentation of his elaborately developed theory. Suffice it to say that the opening of events occurs in the sign of Virgo. Thus, Bullinger's theory implies, without directly saying so, that the true primogeniture of the zodiac—far more ancient than modern interpretation will allow—must apparently lie at a point somewhere in Virgo, rather than 0° Aries (or at a disputed point in Taurus, as the siderealists insist) and that Adamic man must have had his origins within that Virgoan age, namely, somewhere between 13,119 and 10,960 B.C. But this unpublicized aspect of his portrayal of events, which could readily have ruffled the feathers of a great many prominent scientists and theologians of his day, mercifully went unnoticed. Bullinger chose not to draw attention to it, although it could scarcely have escaped his personal awareness. Such a disquieting deduction, actually assigning a celestially oriented time frame for Adam's appearance in the earth, could only be made by looking at Bullinger's armada of evidence through the long-range lens of the 25,920-year precession of the equinoxes. This was not at all his point of focus. Rather, his lineup of celestial and terrestrial data unfolded along the more familiar annual path of the solar ecliptic, thus sidestepping the potential controversy his highly original interpretation of the zodiac could easily have ignited if viewed through the opposite end of the astrological lens. In short, the perspective presented by Bullinger was a "forward" progression through the twelve signs, starting with Virgo and ending with Leo, in keeping with the annual cycle of "birth signs," rather than the reverse order of the Grand Cycle of the Ages.

In the sign of Virgo, Bullinger shows that the name of this sign in the Hebrew is *Bethulah,* which means "a virgin," and in the Arabic, "a branch." This introductory theme is skillfully developed with numerous biblical quotations, moving on to celestial facts. For instance, the first constellation in Virgo is Comah, meaning "the desired," or "the longed for." The more ancient zodiacs, Bullinger tells us, pictured this constellation as a woman with a child in her arms. He specifically cites from the astrological lore of the Persians, the Chaldeans, and the Egyptians to support this interpretation. In fact, in more precise symbolic terms, we learn that the ancient Egyptian name for the constellation of Comah was *Shes-nu,* which translates "desired *son.*"

Next, in the constellation of Boötes (we are still in the sign of Virgo), golden Arcturus is interpreted as meaning "He cometh," alluding to the Christ. (In Edgar Cayce Reading 827–1, we find Arcturus identified as that star which guided the shepherds to Bethlehem, while Reading 900–10 tells us that "the man called Jesus" went on to Arcturus "as of the developing"; so here we have an interesting parallel with Bullinger's scholarly findings.) Within that same constellation, a star in the spearhead of Boötes the Shepherd—"the Coming One"—is *Al Katurops,* meaning "the branch," as well as "treading under foot." *Nekkar,* meaning "the pierced," is another star in this same constellation.

Thus, with scholarly mastery, Bullinger carries us through the various zodiacal signs with their individual stars and asterisms, patiently depicting the Messiah's agonizing journey through the earth and His eventual triumph and Second Coming, with this last phase depicted, of course, in the closing sign of Leo. Here we have the glorious *Orion,* whose foot is coming down on the enemy's head *(Lepus).* And we see *Him* in the Lion of the Tribe of Judah (symbolized by Leo), about to tread down that Old Serpent *Hydra,* the Devil.

Regrettably, as Bullinger's scholarly annotations make abundantly clear, Greek and Latin corruptions inherited as fixtures of modern astronomy and astrology have clouded and nearly obscured the ancient symbolism. But the symbols are there. The story, which is written in the heavens, is as enduring as His Word.

Leaving Bullinger now, we must journey back in time to the generations of the early patriarchs, as given in Genesis. If, as the readings suggest and various extant legends maintain, Enoch and Hermes were one, and if Enoch was indeed a reincarnation of Adam, as given in a number of esoteric sources as well as in the Cayce readings, then how does this serve to pinpoint Adam's appearance in the Age of Virgo?

Quite simple, really.

The Cayce readings introduce Hermes (Enoch) as the master architect of the Great Pyramid, which was supposedly constructed in a one-hundred-year period from 10,490 to 10,390 B.C. (as already mentioned in Chapter 2). Now, the biblical account of the days of Enoch, as found in Genesis, states that they numbered three hundred sixty and five years. Yet, rather than saying that he died, we find this cryptic allusion to a physical "translation" of some kind: "And Enoch walked with God," says the author of

Genesis, "and he *was not;* for God took him." In the aprocryphal Secrets of Enoch,[3] his transition is explained in these mystical terms: "When Enoch had talked to the people, the Lord sent out darkness onto the earth . . . and it covered those men standing with Enoch, and they took Enoch up . . . and light came again."

It is our speculation that Enoch was transported to Egypt—or, more precisely, to the Libyan mount—where the Edgar Cayce readings indicate he joined forces with the exiled priest, Ra Ta, later returning with Ra Ta and his fellow exiles to Egypt. But now, rather than being known as Enoch in this new land, the stranger and teacher in their midst was called Thoth, or Hermes. But that's getting a bit ahead of our story, for his rightful introduction is in our next chapter.

The point, then, is simply this: Enoch's birth, if we count back some 375 or more years from 10,490 B.C., when construction on the Great Pyramid supposedly commenced, was about 10,865 B.C. The patriarch was six generations removed from Adam, yet the span in years was more than six hundred. Finally, in Genesis 5, wherein the generations of Adam are given, we find a serious gap, which can perhaps be attributed to some early biblical censorship on the part of that sect known as the Sethians. For we find the account of Adam's direct progeny beginning with Seth's birth, and Adam's age is suspiciously given as "an hundred and thirty years" at the time, although He was presumably much older. Why? Because omitted from this censored version is any reference to the earlier days of Adam in the Garden of Eden, or the eventual birth of Cain and Abel. Conceivably, we have "lost" as much as several hundred years—perhaps more. (We are not questioning Adam's total length of days, which was given as nine hundred and thirty years, but we suggest that there may have been some "doctoring" by Sethian zealots in assigning to Adam a relatively youthful one hundred and thirty years at the time of Seth's birth, when he was probably considerably older. By this device, no question arises concerning the unaccounted-for centuries of his earlier transgressions, which simply have no place in this expurgated chapter, presumably a separate scroll or palimpsest.) Anyhow, by our estimation, Adam must have had his Edenic beginnings some thousand years or so ahead of Enoch's time, not a mere six hundred. Otherwise, Adam would still have been alive at Enoch's birth—a circumstance contradicted by the Cayce records, as well as legendary accounts cited by Jung and other scholars, which identify Enoch as the first in a series of reincarnations of Adam, leading up to his final entry in the earth as Jesus.

To summarize: In round figures, we would speculate that Adam probably projected into the earth-plane about 12,000 B.C., near the midpoint of the Virgoan age.

Finally, all of this serves to corroborate our theory about the present Great Year cycle, commencing in Virgo and ending in Libra. Amilius, the Maker of the manifest universe—*including the zodiac*—set the pattern for the zodiacal ages when He chose the "Age of the Virgin" to enter His own creation as Adam, the Son of man, during that second influx of souls, coming among His own in flesh-form to take on the predestined role of a Redeemer.

Only one major question remains unanswered, looming in front of us like some Sphinxian riddle: If there is to be a shifting of the poles at the turn of the century (whether a partial tilt or a magnetic reversal, or perhaps a combination, was not stated), how might this affect our planetary relationship to the constellation of Libra? What surprising realignment with the signs of the zodiac could come about with even a minor shifting of the earth's geopolar or magnetic axis? Perhaps we are destined to meet the sign of Judgment a bit ahead of schedule. If so, only time and planetary tilt can tell . . .

5. An Aryan in Egypt

EXODUS FROM ARARAT

Questionings arose. There was much consternation and dispute among the elders. Clearly, the pale-bodied, blue-eyed boy-child represented both an oddity and a threat to the tribe of Zu. For he was not one of them, yet his unique social status demanded full recognition.

His mother, a daughter of Zu, spoke of visitations from the gods of that area, between the Caucasian Mountains and the Caspian Sea, who had brought about his conception.[1] She declared that his name was to be Ra Ta, signifying the first pure white in the earth.[2] Indeed, she spoke of her newborn son with such an unaccustomed air of authority and purpose that some were strangely moved by her words, while others were made uneasy by them.

All knew of her innocence and purity. And none dared to doubt the integrity of her speech, as a daughter of the leader Zu himself. Yet because of the infant's alien appearance and because he had no father from among the tribesmen to claim him and raise him, it was argued by some among the council of elders that the child should be disposed of. Others, however, warned of retribution from higher forces if such a rash act were to be carried out. For in those days, some 10,600 years before the entry of the Prince of Peace into the earth[3] and only a millennium or so after Adam's advent, the gods were not so far removed from the minds or the activities of the sons and daughters of men that they had forgotten to respect and fear them. So it was decided, instead, with Zu's reluctant approval, that the mother and her newborn son should be sent away—rejected, as permanent outcasts from the tribe. However, they were to be accompanied by a small retinue of "things" (those grotesque remnants of unholy cohabitation by the sons of

Belial with the beasts in the earth, who now labored for the sons of men), and these would protect and serve them in their wanderings.

Thus it was that Ra Ta and his mother eventually found their way to the slopes of that mountain now known as Ararat, and named after the Carpathian leader who had established a home community for a band of his nomadic people in that place. It lay in a northwestern quadrant of that land later known as Persia, or the Aryan empire (today within Turkish borders).

King Ararat, marveling at the child's unusual appearance, immediately welcor ied the outcasts to his primitive encampment. He treated them henceforth as his own. Although Ararat condemned Zu's actions, he instinctively sensed that the gods may have had a hand in leading the outcasts into his protective custody for reasons beyond his present comprehension.

The boy Ra Ta grew swiftly, gaining in grace and stature. But that was not all. He began to exhibit an uncanny psychic ability, of which the king took careful note. Often, too, the lad would wander off alone, deep in his trancelike meditations. When asked about these long periods of entering into the silence, Ra Ta reassured the king.

"The gods sometimes speak to me when I am very still," he said matter-of-factly. "It is like a wise voice within me, giving me directions."

The king nodded approvingly.

"That is good, my son," he told him. "Be an attentive listener, then. I believe it is the voice of the Creative Forces that speaks through you, and when you are old enough I shall make you a priest to my people. Then you shall instruct them in the ways of the higher laws, called the Law of One. It is the knowledge all upright men are continually seeking."

Ra Ta was greatly pleased. It was just what the inner voice had told him would be his future destiny.

The king's own son, Arart, was a shepherd in the higher pastures, and somewhat older than Ra Ta. Yet a close bond had developed between them. Arart was skilled in the arts of warfare and politics, but he also sought knowledge of a moral and religious nature, which would make him a wise ruler one day. Ra Ta had a natural understanding of these matters, and whenever he joined Arart in the higher pastures, the future king would sit, entranced, as his younger friend instructed him with ease and grace, answering all manner of ethical and metaphysical questions as if from some inner well of wisdom.

In his twenty-first year, Ra Ta received a prophetic vision.

The vision had come to him as a spiritual directive, and Ra Ta hastened to tell the king about it. It concerned a whole "new order" of things that was even now in the making, and King Ararat's people were chosen to play a decisive role in the unfolding pattern of events, along with Ra Ta. Led by the king's son, Arart, as their new ruler, and with Ra Ta as their spiritual leader and guide, a pioneering group of some nine hundred souls was to journey many moons southward into the land of Egypt. There, with divine help, they would conquer the native inhabitants—peacefully, if at all possible—and set up a new rule in that ancient kingdom, which was materially far advanced though spiritually decadent. Yet Ra Ta's vision nevertheless told him that Egypt marked the spiritual center of the Universal Forces in the earth. From this center there were destined to emanate many spiritual changes and teachings, he explained to the king, that would serve to awaken the then-developing nations and races among the sons and daughters of men so that they could be made aware of their spiritual roots and responsibilities. Without such an awakening, Ra Ta warned King Ararat, mankind could not hope to survive a great planetary cataclysm that was fast approaching. Nor could the necessary preparations be made to preserve the sacred records of the era, as a warning and a revelation to future generations in a distant age, to be uncovered when the proper time had come.

The king gazed intently upon the tall, alabaster-like figure of his newly appointed young priest, with his flowing mane of flaxen hair and eyes the color of azurite. He had listened well to Ra Ta's inspired words, and it took only one look into the impenetrable depths of those strange blue eyes to tell Ararat that he must heed the prophecy. The prospect somewhat saddened him; he would be staying behind, with an aging remnant of his tribe, here on the slopes of the great mountain to which he had first brought his people to establish a home community, while his son now followed his earlier example by leading a great horde of hardy pioneers into yet another distant land.

Ararat might have wondered privately at the choice of Egypt, despite Ra Ta's compelling psychic convictions. Yet according to the readings, it was inevitable. A number of factors made it so:

Why Egypt? This [place] had been determined [by those forces guiding Ra Ta] . . . as the center of the universal activities of nature, as well as the spiritual forces, and where there might be the least disturbance by the convulsive movements which came about in the earth [soon thereafter] through the [final] destruction of Lemuria, Atlantis, and—in later periods —the flood.

When the lines about the earth are considered from the mathematical precisions, it will be found that the center is nigh unto where the Great Pyramid [later to be constructed by Ra and Hermes] . . . is still located.

Then, there were the mathematical, the astrological and the numerological indications, as well as the individual urge [determining Ra Ta's choice of Egypt]. (281–42)

The preceding reference to "the lines about the earth" relates, in all probability, to those esoteric measurements called "ley lines," which are apparently determined in some arcane manner by the positions of the stars. It is believed that prehistoric science had mastered the use of these ley patterns in determining the exact positioning of many sacred structures, such as Stonehenge and the Great Pyramid, which still stand today in mute testimony to an ancient wisdom now forgotten.

As for the "individual urge" prompting Ra Ta, alluded to in the foregoing excerpt, this presumably emanated from his own subconscious memory patterns of that much earlier Egyptian cycle as the androgynous ruler Asapha. Now those old memories were drawing him back to the same general locale that had once before served as a world center for spiritually directed activities, during a similar time of planetary crisis. For, as given, "in the earth manifestation and the cycle of time, much repeats itself."[4]

Preparations for the exodus from Mount Ararat, like the long and perilous journey that lay ahead, took many, many moons. Provisions had to be gathered; slings and other crude weaponry had to be fashioned for the coming battle, as well as for the defense en route and the gathering of fresh game along the way; and fearsome beasts of warfare—including bulls, bears, leopards and hawks—had to be specially trained by Arart's warriors and, in some instances, equipped with cleverly wrought spiked collars to enhance their ferocity.[5] In devising this strategy of fear, Arart reasoned that they could thus subdue their potential enemies more quickly, cowing them into surrender without needless bloodshed. Ra Ta's preferred approach to the Egyptians was that of friendly persuasion, which he planned to use in conjunction with Arart's more forceful tactics. Peace, not war, was Ra Ta's goal. He sought eventual unification of Arart's invading forces not only with those peoples in the Egyptian land but with the tribal clusterings of mankind that were now gathering into the separate nations and races of the prophesied new order, thus bringing about a closer relationship of man to the Creator, and of man to man.

Ra Ta and Arart included in their entourage many of those classless beings termed "things" by the Atlanteans, who now served the sons of men as laborers. However, in the new land toward which they were headed, their subhuman status was to be raised by the priest to that of potential equals who, through purification, "might eventually become channels through which blessings, and knowledge of the divine influence and force, might be made manifest."[6]

The caravan of some nine hundred souls at last departed, as Ra Ta and Arart turned their backs forever upon Mount Ararat. The awesome procession, stretching a mile or more in length, traveled mostly afoot, with beasts of burden taking the place of wagons or carriages.[7] It was to be a long and arduous journey, requiring numerous prolonged encampments en route to replenish their energies as well as their provisions. Yet, across the broad plains and rugged hills of Araby lay a shimmering land of promise and plenty.

Egypt! There the River of Life poured its abundant waters upon the green and fertile delta, and the sun shed its bright rays upon a dark-skinned people whose perennial prosperity had gradually led to indolence and materialism. These were mostly the evolving descendants of Asapha's people, from an age only dimly remembered. Now that same Asapha was returning to his own. They would see in the strange, alabaster-pale figure of the charismatic priest an image of the Sun itself, brought down to earth.

Based upon the readings, it was perhaps an understandable confusion:

[For] the entrance into the Ra Ta experience, when there was the journeying from materiality—or the being translated in materiality as Ra Ta—was from the infinity forces, or from the Sun; with those influences that draw upon the planet itself, the earth and all those about same.

Is it any wonder that in the ignorance of the earth the activities of that entity were [later] turned into that influence called the sun-worshippers? (5755–1)

THE VICTORS AND THE VANQUISHED

King Raai was a man of peace. More than that, the elderly ruler of the Egyptians was a man who chose solitude over pomp and ceremony. He had increasingly isolated himself, of late. The king was by nature a philosopher, and affairs of state bored him. Thus, he had paid less and less attention to governing his people in his declining years, preferring to let them govern themselves. This was not too difficult, fortunately, in a land that was sufficiently prosperous and happy to pose no major problems.

Or so it seemed, at any rate.

Then, one fateful day, Arart and his great horde of fierce-looking tribesmen suddenly descended upon the sleeping city of Luz just as the sun awoke.

Terrified farmers, up early to work in their fields, fled in horror at the sight of the approaching warriors, who were flanked on either side by wild, bloodthirsty beasts straining at their leashes. In the vanguard of the strange procession was a tall, white-bodied figure such as they had never seen before, with both of his hands raised aloft. This was the priestly Ra Ta, signaling them to surrender and make peace.

Make peace they did—not only the farmers encountered along their triumphal route, but the startled populace within the city itself. Only a token resistance occurred at the hands of ill-prepared and badly outnumbered guards outside the royal palace. In the midst of the slaughter, however, King Raai came forth. He ordered a halt to the futile resistance by his own forces. Then he graciously surrendered his rulership to Arart, upon receiving assurances from Ra Ta of the invaders' benevolent purposes in accord with the precepts of the Law of One.

So the new rule began, and Arart was designated the first of the "shepherd kings" from the north. (His son, Araaraart, who was to be born some years later in the new land, would become the second to bear that epithet.[8]) We do not know what symbolic significance such an epithet may have carried, if any, but undoubtedly it bespoke in plain terms the invaders' pastoral origins.

The readings say of Raai's act of submission to Arart's forces that, although condemned at the time by some of his own people, it demonstrated a principle that later became the basis for the studies of the Prince of Peace himself.[9] This was undoubtedly the Christ-like principle of laying self-interest aside for the sake of the greater good.

(In his next incarnation, however, Raai lost. This was during Cayce's Persian cycle as the nomadic ruler, Uhjltd, again playing the role of an invader, while Raai—known as Bestreld then—was the keeper of the exchequer for Croesus. Much of Croesus's fabled wealth was apparently due to Bestreld's greedy hoarding. Yet in the actual sacking of the storehouses by the invading forces, the life reading states that the entity Bestreld finally *gained*, in the material loss encountered and the subsequent persecutions. A curious way to "gain," one might say, but from the karmic aspect, apparently a needed lesson was learned. Thus, it is our speculation that in his previous incarnation as King Raai, the entity may have harbored a secondary reason for his hasty surrender, a reason less noble than the first. In short, he perhaps sought to preserve his worldly goods by this action, as further resistance to Arart's forces would probably have cost him the loss of his possessions, and even his life, in addition to his throne. If our speculation is valid, then it serves to demonstrate in dramatic fashion how closely intertwined are the karmic threads of our lives with those whom we daily encounter. Yet, when Raai once again came on the scene as the present-day entity [1734], and found himself drawn to the former priest Ra Ta, who was now Edgar Cayce, it was for a spiritual opportunity in *both* their lives, and a mutual blessing.)

Back to Egypt and our story.

Among the natives of the land, there dwelt a young scribe and teacher of unusual mental abilities, who was the principal sage of a cult known as the Euranians.[10] He was well versed in the esoteric application of numbers, among other mysteries, and he soon came to King Arart's attention. This compelling young intellectual and occultist, although once removed from power by Arart's fearful predecessor, King Raai, was still much respected among many of the more influential of the native inhabitants and had a considerable though discreet following.

Now that the new rule under Arart was bringing about many important changes in the social, moral, and religious order of the land, the king sensed the need for a prominent figure among the native populace to stand at his side, as it were, as a trusted councillor or scribe who could interpret to his own people the intent and purpose of the new laws and the new rule being formulated by the king and the priest. In this way, the rising tide of resentment and criticism could be deflected. The influential young leader of the Euranians struck Arart as a most logical choice.

And so, in his thirty-second year, the young Egyptian was invited to share in the pomp, glory, and power of Arart's rulership, while occupying a position parallel, in a historical sense, to that of Jefferson in the drafting of the Declaration of Independence. For, as explained in one of the readings for Mr. [900], who had been that chosen scribe and interpreter, "the scribe set about to give those interpretations in the combination as Jefferson gave that of liberty to [the people] . . . [presenting] those truths as pertaining to man's relation with the higher creative energy and forces."[11]

This appointment occurred in the third year of Arart's dynasty. At the time of the invasion of Egypt by Arart's forces,[12] the youthful scribe was only twenty-nine. Moreover, in many parts of the world in those days, the age of male maturity was regarded to be thirty-three. Yet the king himself was probably not much older than that, and Ra Ta, the chosen priest, had been only twenty-one when he first received his psychic inspiration to undertake the entry into Egypt—a journey that we assume may have taken the invading forces a decade or more, considering the slow and deliberate preparations and the long and frequent encampments en route with such a vast entourage. All the same—give or take a decade in our calculations—it may be seen that the "shepherd king" Arart, the priest, and the native scribe were all relatively youthful contemporaries of one another. Consequently, with their combined energies working toward the development of that ideal as set by the priest, this ruling "troika" must have represented a veritable dynamo of spiritual reform in a land that was far more accustomed to its own former leisurely pace and materialistic goals. Inevitably, the rumblings of discontent, particularly among the former ruling class, began to grow. As the years continued to roll by and the level of reform intensified under Ra Ta's unrelenting efforts, replacing the last vestiges of a materialistic and class-conscious culture with a more egalitarian and spiritually based rule, the discontent became increasingly vocal, most notably among the deposed aristocracy, whose special vulnerability made them all the more rebellious. They protested a lack of fair representation.

It was at this time that King Arart made a totally unexpected move. His young son and heir apparent, Araaraart, who had been born in the new land, was now sixteen. A mere stripling! Yet Arart saw that this very fact would work in his favor. He decided to turn over his throne to the boy, and then make the Egyptian scribe, whom he had learned to trust, a full-fledged member of the royal household, assuming "Aarat" as his family name. He then planned to pit Aarat's considerable talents against the new young king's, so to speak, by elevating him to the role of a special councillor to the youthful ruler. It proved to be a clever bit of strategy. The native populace was considerably mollified by this conciliatory gesture, and the various reforms in progress could still proceed as usual. The retiring king reserved a background role for himself, and he was confident, meanwhile, that his son, who was quick of mind and speech despite his tender years, would soon be wise in the ways of power and emerge as an excellent ruler. He was very nearly right. But later on, a flawed judgment intervened.

When he was thirty, Araaraart II, as the second "shepherd king" was called, surveyed the political situation about him and made what appeared to be an astute decision. In part, perhaps, to undercut some of the entrenched influence of his native adviser, Aarat, but also to create the semblance of a more democratic rule, the young king formed a cabinet, or council, of twelve advisers,[13] drawing their numbers impartially from among the native populace as well as his own people. These twelve, in consultation with one another and with the king, would aid in deciding the affairs of state. However, for the crucial position of chief councillor, Araaraart II retained a somewhat Machiavellian figure named Asriaio, who was of his father's people from the north and had been chief councillor in his father's court.

Although these developments appeared to offer expanded representation of the people's interests in the royal court, they also gave the young king ample leverage against his Egyptian rival, Aarat, whose voice would henceforth be only one among twelve. Yet it was a move that was to work against the king's interests in the end, as he tended to listen more and more to the advice of others rather than to his own inner voice.

Ra Ta, the high priest, was to be another loser from Araaraart's political manipulations.

In the beginning, the choosing of Ra Ta as high priest in the new land, with supreme authority over the native people as well as Arart's people in all matters religious or spiritual had met with jealous resistence and much dissension in certain ruling quarters. This highly vocal opposition had gradually been silenced, however, as the inspired nature of the priest's psychic powers became more and more evident even to his most vociferous opponents. At last they no longer dared speak out against him. The priest's programs of moral and spiritual reform had gradually made Ra Ta a figure of awe and veneration among the masses. His success was epitomized in the extraordinary results of the purification rituals in the Temple of Sacrifice, where the "things" were being cleansed of such bestial hindrances as the cloven hoof or tails or feathers, among other monstrosities and protuberances, and the Temple Beautiful, where those souls purified in the physical could then go for mental and spiritual training to fit them for higher service to God and man. By some, in their ignorance, the priest was even viewed as a god himself.

The Egyptians, in their cultural advancement over Arart's more pastoral and simple tribesmen, had long enjoyed lighter-than-air travel in gas-laden balloons introduced to them by the Atlanteans in times past. And now that Atlantean evacuees were beginning to arrive in increasing numbers, as their priests and priestesses warned of the impending destruction of Poseidia, and strife with the sons of Belial was accelerating, Ra Ta saw an opportunity to visit other areas of the world where the sons of men were gathered. So he went to India, to the Gobi land, to Og, and to what is now Peru, as well as to Carpathia, speaking to the spiritual leaders in these places about the evolving new order of things and the preparations for the new root race then emerging. Also, he went to the fair city of Alta, in Poseidia, where he conferred with many of the children of the Law of One. One of the leaders there, a great sage named Hept-supht, chose to come to Egypt and assist the priest in the great reforms he was undertaking with the peoples in that land. For he knew, as did Ra Ta, that Egypt was to become a great spiritual center in the days immediately ahead and a place where the records must be preserved, even as was being done in Atlantis already and would be done later by Iltar in Yucatan.[14]

As these more esoteric activities were proceeding in the spiritual affairs of the land, Egypt was also experiencing dramatic developments in commerce and construction and the arts. Under the supervision of Ararat I, and later his son and successor, Araaraart II, mining activities were aggressively pursued in a search for precious stones and gems, as well as such minerals as zinc, copper, tin, and the like. The construction of temples and other edifices went forward relentlessly. Storehouses became commonplace and served as places of exchange or barter in international commerce with merchants from other lands. Egypt was thriving.

It was thriving, but not everyone was happy. Many of the former pleasures had been outlawed by the priest. And his increasingly frequent absences as he journeyed to other parts of the planet to confer with spiritual leaders, became occasions to revive those sinful self-indulgences forbidden by Ra Ta. The concocting of intoxicating brews was one, and another was the sexual abuse of those poor, victimized "things" who were undergoing the various stages of purification and higher development in the Temple of Sacrifice and the Temple Beautiful.

The priest, upon returning unexpectedly from a regional archaeological expedition, learned firsthand of these violations of his edicts, and, to put the matter in common parlance, "all hell broke loose." Moreover, the violations were not only being committed by certain disgruntled native subjects but also by some of Araaraart's own clansmen. Ra Ta went to the council with his complaints.

But what the priest did not know, in his innocently trusting nature, was that several among the councillors themselves were on the side of the lawbreakers. This included the chief councillor, Asriaio, who had succumbed to the evil machinations of Ra Ta's enemies as they sought some way to discredit and overthrow the priest. It was mankind's first conflict between Church and State.

When the Devil can find no other way to get a man, he sends for a woman. And this is what the plotters did.

One of Ra Ta's edicts was that no man should have more than one wife. At the same time, his obsession with developing as many representatives as possible of the emerging white race he himself embodied was well known, for the changing of the pigmentation to lighter hues—though an act not wholly in accord with spiritual purposes, as will be shown in a later chapter—was one of the more remarkable accomplishments Ra Ta had presumably learned from the Atlanteans and had been applying with varying degrees of success in the developmental phases in the Temple of Sacrifice and, later, the Temple Beautiful. Indeed, so eager was he to hasten the law of evolution that it had become a blind spot, as it were, in his own understanding and application of the spiritual laws governing such matters. For the hand of God is seldom hurried, and racial differences served a definite purpose in the Divine Plan.

Knowing the priest's one weakness, then, the plotters moved to exploit it. In the Temple Beautiful was a dancer named Isris, whose fairness of skin and unusual grace and beauty had made her an object of envy and desire by many. The daughter of the second sacrificial priest, she was a special favorite of the young king, Araaraart II. If she could be persuaded that a liaison with the priest would serve a good cause, in producing a truly perfect offspring from their mating, the next step would be relatively easy: one glance from the eye of Isris, followed by the appropriate words, and the priest would be fair game for the plotters' evil arrow.

It worked, of course, as expected. (As an aside, though, Isris's karmic payoff in the present life was near-blindness in one eye.)

When a daughter was born nine months later from the illicit union of Ra Ta and Isris, all that remained was to spring the trap that would convict the offending priest of violating his own edict. The matter went before the king for judgment. Araaraart, who was perhaps less enraged by Ra Ta's infidelity to his own law than by the fact that his favorite dancer, Isris, had been involved as a partner in the sexual transgression, was readily persuaded that Ra Ta should be punished. The question was whether to put him to death, as certain extremists among his councillors recommended, or to seek some less drastic means of meting out kingly displeasure upon the hapless priest.

The banishment of both offenders was urged upon Araaraart by his chief councillor, Asriaio. It was seconded by Aarat the Egyptian.

Thus it came to pass that Ra Ta was sent into exile, accompanied by some 231 souls who remained loyal to him. This included the Atlantean sage, Hept-supht, and the priest's favorite daughter, Aris-Hobeth, whose name meant "Favored One." Both were to be a great comfort to him, along with the sorrowfully repentant Isris, in the years of trial that lay ahead of the priest in the far Nubian mount of their exile.

As for the fair child, Iso, that luckless offspring of the fatal union between Ra Ta and Isris, the vengeful king held her as a hostage. Though well cared for, she was to die of desolation before the exile period ended. The reading for this soul-entity, known as [288], indicated that she was that twin soul of Edgar Cayce's whom the reader has already encountered in earlier chapters.

Meanwhile, as the priest and his party of fellow exiles journeyed southward under a blazing Egyptian sun, Ra Ta reflected ruefully upon the far-reaching and tragic consequences of his momentary weakness. And as he looked toward the purple hills of Nubia that lay ahead, forbidding and mysterious in their bleak majesty, he thought he could hear echoing ever so faintly at his back the mocking laughter of the gods.

THE PRIEST IN EXILE

The Cayce readings on the Ra Ta period refer interchangeably to the place of exile as the "Nubian" or the "Libyan" mount, while the local inhabitants are similarly spoken of as either Libyans or Nubians. Also there is at least one reference to Abyssinia as the general setting. The latter, of course, is today known as Ethiopia; it lies directly below Egypt and the Sudan. Nubia, which no longer exists as a separate country, is now remembered only for the Nubian Desert, in the eastern sector of northern Sudan, just above the northernmost tip of Ethiopia. Thus, it seems likely, in view of the language of the readings, that all of this general area was once a part of the ancient Libyan kingdom—with the Nubian principality occupying only that small, easternmost sector of

Libya's vast desert empire—to which Ra Ta and his band of fellow exiles were either specifically sent at Araaraart's command or voluntarily chose to go.

More probably the latter. We say this in light of the unique associations awaiting them there, which suggest that Ra Ta was again being guided by his psychic promptings. As far as the king's wishes were concerned, we submit that the terms of exile may only have required that the priest be banished to a place outside the borders of Egypt. But if the kingdom of Libya was indeed the king's mandate—and admittedly, Reading 294–151 does say, "to Libya were these people sent"—one may suspect that the selection of the Nubian mount, at least, was Ra Ta's.

In support of this supposition, there is a vital clue to be found in Reading 294–148, suggesting that Ra Ta may already have been familiar with that same mount of exile in the Nubian hills. Although no geographical indicator is included in this particular reference, which would clearly confirm the suspicion, the reading alludes to Ra Ta's return from "one of those visits to the mount." Moreover, it concerns a period immediately prior to Ra Ta's betrayal, when he first discovered evidence of lustful activities and other acts of self-aggrandizement by those in charge in the Temple of Sacrifice. What would have been more natural, then, when the priest found himself sent into a Libyan exile than to return to that same mount where he had so recently been meditating and researching?

The nature of that research, which had apparently been going on for some while, was "delving into what was termed the archaeological conditions of those that had lived in the lands in the periods before,"[15] and remembering that Ra Ta had reigned in Upper Egypt, as Asapha, during a much earlier incarnation, he undoubtedly experienced psychic recall of the whole general area and its ancient inhabitants, over whom he had presumably ruled. In summary, then, the basic nature of Ra Ta's archaeological research appears to have been at the *psychic* level first, even as was to be the case ages later when he reincarnated as a twentieth-century prophet and seer, Edgar Cayce, and gave psychic readings that

were to become the basis for much highly promising archaeological research work that still continues in the Middle East and
other areas of the world (and may one day be resumed in Iran).

Returning to the days of Ra Ta, here is a revealing reference to
the priest's early psychic pronouncements, or "readings," as we
would term them, during the initial period of Arart I's rule in the
conquered Egyptian kingdom:

> With Ra Ta then beginning with the natives and *those that listened to the
> uncovering of the records* (in what would be termed archaeological research
> in the present), gradually more and more adherence was made to those
> words of this peculiar leader that had come into this land. (294–147; italics
> added)

Whatever setback Ra Ta may have experienced as the deposed
high priest in Egypt, there were now compensatory blessings in
the Nubian land:

> With the entering into the Nubian land, there came such a change that
> there were the bettered conditions in every term that may be applied to
> human experience. . . . As the priest in this period entered more and more
> into the closer relationships with the Creative Forces, greater were the
> abilities for the entity or body Ra Ta to be able to make or bring about the
> *material* manifestations of that relationship. Hence the peace that was en-
> joyed by the peoples, not only with the priest but all those of that land.
> (294–150)

Also, some very interesting activities were begun. Some of their
effects, surprisingly, are still with us in the present:

> There were begun some memorials in the Nubian land which still may
> be seen, even in this period, in the mountains of the land. Whole moun-
> tains were honeycombed, and were dug into sufficient to where the per-
> petual fires are *still* in activity in these various periods, when the priest
> then began to show the manifestations of those periods of reckoning the
> longitude (as termed now), latitude, and the activities of the planets and
> stars, and the various groups of stars, constellations, and the various influ-
> ences that are held in place, or that *hold* in place those about this particular
> solar system. Hence in the Nubian land there were first begun the reckon-
> ing of those periods when the Sun has its influence upon human life, and

let's remember that it is [was?] in this period when the *present race* has been called into being—and the *influence* is reckoned from all experiences of Ra Ta, as the effect upon the body physical, the body mental, the body spiritual, or soul body. (294–150)

Here it may be useful to pause, and ask ourselves what Cayce meant in the preceding excerpt, in referring to "this period when the *present race* has been called into being." The answer seems to revolve around a simple question of syntax—one of the recurrent hazards, admittedly, in working with the Cayce readings. If the phrase "this period" alludes to Ra Ta's era, not ours (and I think it must), then the reference was undoubtedly to the fourth root race —our own, in fact, and thus the "present race"—at a time when the Adamic Age was still in its infancy. However, mankind is now on the threshold of yet another transformation, which will introduce a new root race, which Cayce has identified as the fifth. But this new development cannot yet be termed the "present race," for it is not yet fully upon us. We are told that its actual beginnings are to be signaled by an event that may still lie a full generation ahead of us: the opening of a concealed Pyramid of Records, buried under the Gizeh complex, somewhere between the mysterious Sphinx and the Nile. (This matter will be taken up in proper detail later in the chapter.)

To continue, then, we find that Ra Ta's esoteric activities in the Nubian land involved all manner of celestial observations and scientific inquiry that form a part of our present heritage.

Of special significance to the researcher in a correlation of Ra Ta's activities with the much later psychic revelations of Edgar Cayce is the uncanny emphasis always given by Cayce to the role of the Sun, the Moon, the stars and the various constellations, not only in their combined effects upon human life, but upon other life-forms as well, and upon planet Earth itself. In fact, in addition to special readings on the subject, every life reading given by Edgar Cayce can be found to include certain astrological reference points in the past and present soul development of that particular entity. Planetary sojourns elsewhere within our own solar system are also mentioned as a part of each soul's experience in the spiritual plane between earthly incarnations. Finally, it is indicated in the Cayce readings that upon completion of its cycle of development within this solar system, the soul-entity moves on, either through Arcturus or Polaris, for higher development in other spheres of consciousness. (All of this esoteric wisdom, whether or not one is prepared to accept the validity of such arcane revelations, apparently came to Cayce in trance-state as a direct outgrowth of his former psychic development as Ra Ta, in the Nubian land.)

The Nubians were a warlike people. Hostility was their natural reaction, therefore, when the high priest of the Egyptian kingdom to the north, whose previous visits to their hills on relatively brief archaeological missions had involved only a small team of helpers, now very suddenly arrived with a multitude of followers and proceeded to establish a home community in exile, choosing a prominent hilltop where the priest's earlier excavations had taken place. Such bold actions were viewed as a threat, at first.

Yet it did not take long for the charismatic priest to win them over by precept and example, as his enlightened teachings took root and brought manifold blessings to the Nubians, as well as to his own people. Among Ra Ta's first converts was a prince of the Nubian land, who was to be one of many among the native inhabitants to accompany the priest and his people on their triumphal return to Egypt some nine years later.

Another important convert was a seventeen-year-old Libyan princess, named Ai-Si, who was also destined to follow Ra Ta back to Egypt. There she became a musician and priestess in the Temple Beautiful and a drawer of "life seals" depicting the key symbols of a soul-entity's unfolding evolutionary pattern in the earth.

Meanwhile, temples of worship were built in the mount and separate abodes where those who chose to live in pairs, as man and wife, could raise their families. This was a distinct departure from the custom in Egypt, where the life-style was strictly communal, and segregated, women from men, except for periods of union in the conjugal chambers. This creation of a "home life" for his people, as Ra Ta had observed in certain of the lands he had visited, brought a new sense of happiness, prosperity, and peace.

Word of Ra Ta's remarkable accomplishments not only reached King Araaraart's ears in Egypt, where the Ruler's heart was already troubled by private feelings of remorse, but those in distant lands soon heard and came seeking.

One of these was the great initiate, Hermes.

Tradition ascribes to Hermes various sobriquets. Generally known to the Egyptians as Thoth, or Thoth-Hermes, the Greeks later gave him the legendary name of Hermes Trismegistus, meaning "thrice great." To the ancient Egyptians, he was the "scribe of the gods," and "lord of divine words"; he was also regarded as "the heart and the tongue of Ra." But to really pierce his identity, we must revert to a little-known Islamic legend, chronicled by îbn Batuta in A.D. 1352, claiming that Hermes was none other than the patriarch Enoch (known as Idrîs to Muslim scholars), and that *it was he who built the Great Pyramid.* In the apocryphal literature, we find ample evidence to support the view that Enoch, who was apparently translated from the sight of his own people in his three hundred sixty-fifth year, when "God took him,"[16] actually spent many additional decades traveling to the four quarters of the earth, warning the people of cataclysmic changes approaching and the need to draw closer to God. It was he, in fact, who is believed to have warned Noah some few centuries later of an impending flood.

The Edgar Cayce readings, as already noted in an earlier chapter, identify Enoch as an incarnation of the Master, whose immediately prior appearance in the earth had been as Adam. But it may be even more surprising to some to learn that there are in existence certain ancient scholarly sources, cited by both C. G. Jung and Manly P. Hall in some of their writings,[17] wherein Adam and Enoch and Jesus are presented as one and the same entity in different incarnatons. Another incarnation mentioned, further confirming the Cayce readings, is that of the priest-king Melchizedek, who appeared to the patriarch Abraham; but that is another story.

The synonymity between Enoch and Hermes was eventually

uncovered by some of those close to Edgar Cayce. The readings had made repeated allusions to Hermes as an incarnation of the Master, most notably in Reading 281–10, in response to a series of questions by Miss [69]. She was told of her association, as Isaholli, with the Master during the Egyptian period. Since she had attended the priest in his period of exile, when Hermes first appeared among them, the inference seemed logical: Hermes and the Master were one. And although his role at the time seems to be shrouded in mystery, it was undoubtedly significant.

In Reading 69–1, we find what appears to be an elusive reference to Hermes as, simply, "the teacher": "The entity [69] among those who waited on the holy place from which the ministration of that given as moral, penal, and spiritual precept, that both from the priest and *the teacher* of that period" (italics added). But in Reading 281–43, it is more plainly given: there it refers to "what the Teacher of teachers taught" in Egypt.

Hermes was later to accompany the exiles upon their return to Egypt, where the readings tell us that he was the master architect of the Great Pyramid. It should not surprise us that the Master of masters had such a pivotal role in its construction; called the Pyramid of Understanding, it was designed as a temple of initiation, to which Hermes would return in a later age as Jesus, undergoing His youthful initiation with John the Baptist under the supervision of the Essenes, preparing himself for His sacrificial role. So, at least, the readings tell us . . .

To further confirm our identification of the "Teacher of teachers"—that obvious sobriquet for the Master—with Hermes, there is a second reference in Reading 69–1; Isaholli's role, upon the return to Egypt, is given as "the active agent between the king and *the teacher* and the minister [i.e., the priest]" (italics added).

Long were the years of exile; and as messengers from Egypt brought to Ra Ta word of increasing turmoil and strife among the native Egyptians and Araaraart's people, with many added troubles from the rapidly accelerating influx of Atlanteans fleeing from their doomed homeland, the strain upon the priest was great. He who had come into Egypt with an inspired vision and a purpose now feared that all of his earlier accomplishments would come to naught as the result of the discord and divisiveness that had arisen in his prolonged absence. His sorrows were further increased by word of the death of his infant daughter, Iso, who had been held hostage by the vindictive king.

Despite the visible blessings from the continuation, here in the Nubian mount, of the work he had begun decades earlier in Egypt, Ra Ta yearned for a reconciliation with his own people, and also with the young king who had sent him into banishment. He and his present companion, Isris, had paid dearly for their indiscreet union, which the priest had innocently viewed at the time as an acceptable means of serving the development of the new race. He now acknowledged to himself that he had been mistaken, although the punishment had surely been disproportionate to the crime. After all, the law he had been tricked into breaking was not the king's law but his own, as high priest.

In the ninth year of exile, when word finally reached Ra Ta that the king had revoked his order of banishment, and that the priest was to be fully pardoned and restored to his former position of supreme spiritual authority, it was a moment of bittersweet triumph for "this poor, decrepit outcast,"[18] as we find him described at the time.

The priest's followers greeted the news with mixed emotions. Many of them, in fact, had established close ties of a familial nature with the Nubians and would be loath to leave. Moreover, the king's pardon had come only as the result of tediously drawn-out negotiations between the two camps, and now it might have arrived too late. For their leader was now more than one hundred years old. Those closest to Ra Ta, who had observed his increasing frailty, were concerned lest he fail to survive. It would be a great tragedy indeed if he should lack the strength or will, in his hour of final vindication and victory, to draw a divided people together again and lead them back to the Law of One.

But if others doubted the priest's recuperative powers, there was one who did not. That was the ancient sage and teacher Hermes.